GOOD NEWS STUDIES

Consulting Editor: Robert J. Karris, O.F.M.

Volume 31

In the Light of the Lamb

Imagery, Parody, and Theology
in the Apocalypse of John

by

Sophie Laws

Michael Glazier
Wilmington, Delaware

About the Author

Sophie Laws was educated at Oxford University, where she earned the degrees of B.A., M.A., and B. Litt. She was a lecturer in Theology at the University of Leeds from 1968-1969, and at King's College, University of London, from 1969-1982. Among her publications is *A Commentary on the Epistle of James.*

First published in 1988 by Michael Glazier, Inc., 1935 West Fourth Street, Wilmington, Delaware 19805.

Library of Congress Cataloging-in-Publication Data

Laws, Sophie.
    In the light of the lamb.

    Bibliography: p.
    Includes index.
    1. Bible. N.T. Revelation--Criticism, interpretation, etc. I. Title.
BS2825.2.L29   1988   228'.06   87-82348
ISBN 0-89453-639-7 (pbk.)

Typography by Phyllis Boyd LeVane
Printed in the United States of America.

Table of Contents

Foreword

This book represents the public lectures delivered at John Carroll University in Cleveland, Ohio, during my tenure there of the Walter and Mary Tuohy Chair of Interreligious Studies. The lectures are published as they were given, with a few small additions and amendments. It was a great delight to me to come to John Carroll University on my first visit to the United States, and an honour to have been invited to hold the Tuohy Chair. On the publication of the lectures I should like to express my thanks again to the President of the University, the Rev. Thomas O'Malley, S.J., to the Department of Religious Studies and its Chairman the Rev. Kevin O'Connell, S.J., who invited me, and especially to Dr. Joseph Kelly, Director of the Tuohy Chair, who did so much to smooth my path and who gave to me and my family the generous hospitality of his own home.

The book is dedicated to Margaret Grace, my daughter and fellow-pilgrim.

Introduction

In 1966 friends of the late Walter Tuohy, a Cleveland industrialist, established at John Carroll University the Walter and Mary Tuohy Chair of Interreligious Studies, in honor of Mr. Tuohy and his wife, who were both interested in ecumenical activities. The Tuohy Chair has brought to the campus distinguished scholars to discuss topics of interreligious interest; in the 1984-85 academic year our guest was Mrs. Sophie Laws of King's College, London, and her topic was the Apocalypse, a book, which as she notes in her first lecture, has long been a source of controversy among Christians.

Mrs. Laws not only gave the public lectures which are published here; she also gave an undergraduate and a graduate class, both much appreciated by the students. She was also active in a variety of departmental functions, and we in the Department of Religious Studies were glad to have her as a colleague. Since the Tuohy Chair provided Mrs. Laws with her first visit to the United States, we were also happy to welcome, from time to time, her husband, her parents, and her daughter who joined her for the semester.

All of us at John Carroll University hope that Mrs. Laws' first visit to us will not be her last. She brought grace and charm to the Tuohy Chair and, as the lectures will show, scholarship and lucidity to that most difficult of biblical books; we should be happy to have her with us again.

Joseph F. Kelly
John Carroll University

1

Apocalypse and History

The subject of these lectures is a singularly inappropriate one for the Tuohy Chair. The intention of Mrs. Mary Tuohy was eirenic: to found a Chair in "Interreligious Studies," in the first place interdenominational, and also reaching out to non-Christian religions. The Apocalypse, or Revelation, of John has, however, provoked sharply divided views within Christendom; in the Patristic period between East and West: the West, as represented by Irenaeus and Tertullian, early and unreservedly accepting it in their canon as prophecy;[1] the Alexandrian East of Origen and his disciples Eusebius and Dionysius deeply unhappy about its presence and deploring those who "reject the labour of thinking" by taking its promises of the future literally (Origen, *De Principiis* II.xi.1f);[2] the Church in Syria apparently

[1]The Apocalypse of John is also included, with the Apocalypse of Peter, in the Muratorian Canon, a deliberately exclusive list commonly regarded as representing the scripture of the Roman Church ca. A.D. 200.

[2]Eusebius drew up his list of the New Testament scriptures in three categories: those acknowledged, those disputed but familiar to most, and those to be regarded as spurious; and he places the Apocalypse both in the first and the third. His own clear preference is to regard it as spurious, but he cannot deny that it is generally familiar and so deserves to be in the first rank (*Historia Ecclesiastica* III.25.1-7). Dionysius subjected the book to a remarkable critical analysis, demonstrating its difference in style, language and ideas from the gospel of John (Eusebius, *H.E.* VII.24-25). This rejection of its apostolic authorship undoubtedly also throws its authority into question, although Dionysius himself disavows such an intention.

reading it not at all.[3] Since second century Montanism it has, of course, been a book beloved of sectarian or fringe churches, and perhaps for that reason regarded with circumspection if not indeed suspicion by the larger denominations. It was one of the only three books in the New Testament on which the prolific John Calvin wrote no commentary (the other two being 2 and 3 John, for which he might well be excused), while Martin Luther, in the preface to the book in his 1522 translation of the New Testament, declared that his "spirit cannot accommodate itself to this book," and he could not regard it as prophetic or apostolic since it was so full of visions and dreams; indeed he concluded "Christ is neither taught nor known in it."[4]

In the realm of the imagination, too, the Apocalypse evokes sharply contrasted responses. On the one hand, sensibilities recoil from images of martyrs who call for vengeance (6:9f.); of a redeemer who rides spattered with blood (19:13); of blood flowing up to horses' bridles (14:20); of men who gnaw their tongues in unrelievable pain (15:20); indeed from a book in which the love of God or of Christ is only mentioned twice (1:5, 3:9). Yet, on the other hand, the Apocalypse has been the inspiration of much Christian liturgy and culture, in forms as various as the four-square, well-fleeced lamb of the Van Eyck polyptych at Ghent which has adorned countless Easter cards, and as the glorious closing chorus "Worthy is the Lamb" of Handel's *Messiah*.

It is with the Apocalypse as imaginative creation that we shall be primarily concerned, and with those images that Luther so

---

[3]It is wholly absent from the writings of Antiochene scholars like Theodore of Mopsuestia, and does not appear in the Syriac textual tradition of the New Testament until the Philoxenian version, a translation of the New Testament from Greek into Syriac made in 508.

[4]By the time he published his longer preface to the book, in 1530, Luther has however reconciled himself to it to some extent: he finds arguments for regarding it as prophetic, provides a guide to its interpretation, and approves its wholesome assurance that "through and beyond all plagues, beasts, and evil angels Christ is nonetheless with his saints, and wins the final victory" (translation from Vol. 35 of *Luther's Works: Word and Sacrament I*, ed. E.T. Bachman, Philadelphia, 1960, pp. 398-99 for the 1522 preface and 399-411 for the 1530 preface.

mistrusted. In his vision of the heavenly city John wrote that it "has no need of sun or moon to shine upon it, for the glory of God is its light, and its lamp is the Lamb" (21:23). [All quotations are from the Revised Standard Version of the Bible.] Light gives radiance, but it also casts shadow and throws objects into relief; and so imagery may be parody. The aim of these lectures is to show how the great central image of the Lamb serves to interpret and give content to some of the major themes of the book, so that they are seen, for good or ill, "in the light of the Lamb." First, however, there must be some explanation of the presuppositions upon which the Apocalypse will be discussed: first, that as a document it can be classified according to literary genre; and secondly, that as a document it was written in a specific historical setting.

So far as genre goes, the Revelation of John stands in the New Testament as the book of Daniel does in the Old Testament, as an example of apocalyptic literature; indeed it gave to the genre its name, in its self-defining introduction as *apokalupsis Iēsou Christou* (1:1). Apocalyptic, or apocalypticism, is a genre of literature which arose in Judaism in the second century B.C. and which has at its heart the expression of a deep dissatisfacton with the present world-order and a concentration of hope upon a radically different future. So far as defining the precise characteristics of apocalyptic, let the scholar beware! It is a case of *quot homines tot sententiae,* and it has been justly observed that no one apocalypse exhibits all the characteristics which scholars attribute to the group. But there are some generally agreed characteristics of apocalyptic that the Revelation of John can readily be seen to share.[5]

First, the seer regards the time of which he speaks as that for which divine intervention is imminent; it is the time of crisis.

---

[5] Recent studies of apocalyptic include H.H. Rowley, *The Relevance of Apocalyptic,* revised edn. London, 1963; D.S. Russell, *The Method and Message of Jewish Apocalyptic,* London, 1964; P. Vielhauer in E. Hennecke and W. Schneemelcher, *New Testament Apocrypha* II, London, 1965, pp. 581-600; K. Koch, *The Rediscovery of Apocalyptic,* London, 1972; P.D. Hanson, ed., *Visionaries and their Apocalypses,* Philadelphia, 1983; and C. Rowland, *The Open Heaven,* London, 1982.

What he sees is what "must soon take place" (1:1), and "the time is near" (1:3); the martyrs must wait for only "a little longer" for vengeance (6:11); in the course of the vision it is announced by an angel that "there should be no more delay" (10:6); and even the devil's "time is short" (12:12). In the conclusion it is reiterated that what has been shown is what "must soon take place," with the promise "I am coming soon" (22:6f., 12, 20).

Secondly, his perspective is universal: the vision takes in not just the Christian community and its imminent crisis, but the whole world. The four horsemen released in 6:1-8 with their dreadful threats of invasion, civil war, famine and plague, are given authority over one quarter of the earth (v. 8); when the four angels blow their trumpet blasts in 8:7-12, one third of the natural elements, earth, water and stars, suffer, and in 9:13, at the sixth trumpet, one third of mankind. When Babylon falls, it is the nations, their kings and merchants, who witness and lament her fate (18:9-19).

Thirdly, as John's perspective is universal, it is also two-dimensional, taking in both earth and heaven. In the apocalyptic vision of Daniel the earthly conflict between Israel and Syria is associated with the conflict between Michael and the angelic "prince" of Israel and the "princes" of Persia and Greece (10:13, 20f., 12:1); and at Qumran the vision of the war between the sons of light and the sons of darkness is of a war waged by both men and angels (1QM, the *War Rule,* 1, 12, and 17). So in the Apocalypse of John there is both "war in heaven" with angelic armies engaged (12:7-9) and "war" against the saints on earth (13:7), and the final hope is of both "a new heaven and a new earth" (21:1).

Finally, and most obviously, as with other apocalyptic, John's vision is presented with a copious use of elaborate and often bizarre imagery and cryptic symbol, like that of the many-headed and horned beast of 13:18, with his cryptic number-name which the reader is encouraged to decipher (v. 18), and of the great harlot who rides the beast in 17:3ff., whose name is also given as a "mystery" (v. 5).

There is no doubt, broadly speaking, in which category of biblical literature the Apocalypse belongs, and it may be that a consciousness of its genre will help us in approaching one major puzzle of the book: that of its structure. The initial impression is of a document written according to a clearly ordered plan. There is

(1) an introduction and opening vision by John of Christ the revealer (1:1-20), which also introduces the seven churches (v. 20); then

(2) a series of letters to these seven churches (2:1-3:22), the last of which refers to the throne of God (3:21); after which

(3) the seer is taken up into heaven, to see the throne of God and the seven-sealed scroll which he holds (4:1-5:14);

(4) the seven seals are progressively opened, with accompanying disasters (6:1-8:1). Despite the interruption of a long pause between the opening of the sixth and seventh seals (7:1-17), there seems to be a sequence leading to a climax, and we expect that when the seventh seal is opened and the scroll itself unbound, we shall see God's purpose revealed and accomplished. Instead, however, nothing happens: "there was silence in heaven for about half an hour" (8:1). Then begins

(5) a further sequence of seven, this time of angels blowing trumpets, which produces more disasters (8:2-11:19). There is another interruption to the sequence, in the pause between the blowing of the sixth and seventh trumpets (10:1-11:14), but once again we expect a climax, especially as we are told that with the seventh trumpet call "the mystery of God ... should be completed" (10:7), and that "the kingdom of the world has become the kingdom of our Lord and of his Christ" (11:15). Instead, however,

(6) we are confronted with a new set of images, of the dragon and the two beasts, and of heavenly and earthly conflict (12:1-14:20). Again the kingdom is said to pass to God and Christ (12:10), but instead of seeing this kingdom there begins

(7) another series of seven, the seven bowls of wrath, which bring yet more disasters (15:1-16:21). We are told "It is done!" (16:17), but then

(8) we return to the beast, and to the harlot who rides him and who is also the great city (17:1-19:5).

(9) With the fall of Babylon, we are shown the redeemer

victorious over his earthly enemies (19:6-21), and the heavenly adversary is bound (20:1-3), but even then there intervenes the millennial kingdom (20:4-6) and a final eruption of evil (20:7-15) before

(10) the new heaven and earth are established (21:1–22:5), with the final declaration "It is done!" (21:6);

(11) the book concludes with an epilogue, recalling the terms of the introduction (22:6-21): it has been the testimony of Jesus to the churches, delivered to the John who saw and heard it (vv. 8, 16).

There are clearly problems in understanding the sequence of the book; in particular it is difficult to take it as a simple chronological sequence, an unrolling of the map of the future, if only because of the different times that we are told, effectively, that "it is finished," but yet the story goes on (11:5, 12:10, 16:17). Some commentators resort to theories of textual dislocation or the imperfect conflation of sources to explain the apparent disintegration of the initial sense of order. It is possible, however, to suggest relationships between different parts of the pattern, based on the characteristics of the book as apocalyptic which we have already noted.

First, we have three cycles of disaster, those of the seals and the trumpets (stages 4 and 5 in the above outline), and that of the bowls of wrath (stage 7). They differ from each other in that the first two are limited in their scope, affecting one quarter and one third of the world respectively, while the third is total disaster, affecting the whole of the sea, the rivers and the sun. The first two, again, are each "interrupted," to allow for the deliverance of the martyrs; the third runs its course without pause, and blessing has already been pronounced on those "who die in the Lord" (14:13). We may suggest that the first two cycles of disaster are distinct from the third in that they are the preliminary woes of apocalyptic imagination, the universal convulsions that signal the nearness of the end, though "the end is not yet" (cf. Mark 13:3-8), while the third cycle represents the judgment that is part of the end itself: these are the last plagues "for with them the wrath of God is ended" (15:1; cf. the final cosmic convulsions that are part of the end itself in Mark 13:24-27). It is appropriate that it is one of the seven angels who have emptied the bowls of wrath who takes the seer beyond the final judgment into the New Jerusalem in 21:9ff.

Secondly, it may still be asked why there should be two cycles of preliminary or premonitory disaster; but again there is a difference to be noted between them. The seals cycle (stage 4) describes disasters which all emanate on earth, the human catastrophes of war, famine, plague and martyrdom, and the literally earthly catastrophe of earthquake. The trumpets cycle (stage 5) describes disasters which emanate from heaven, hail and fire, a falling fiery mountain, the falling star called "Wormwood," the falling angel of the bottomless pit who is called"Abaddon" or "Apollyon," and the four destroying angels bound at the river Euphrates. This distinction between the two cycles makes sense in terms of the two-dimensional vision of apocalyptic: earth and heaven are alike involved in the great tribulation that signals the end, as they are also in its resolution. The two cycles are therefore not two separate cycles, but a double cycle, each complementary to the other.

Between this double cycle of preliminary disaster and the cycle of final judgment, then, there intervenes the vision of the dragon and the two beasts (stage 6), imagery which returns after the final cycle (stage 8); and a third question is of the relation of these two sections to the rest of the sequence. The imagery drawn on, with the dragon, the great deep and the woman with child, is to a large extent that of creation mythology, though not simply that of the biblical creation myth of Genesis 1 and 2. It is the function of myth to interpret experience and to give expression to what is believed to be its true nature. For example, if men perceive and experience their world as alien or hostile, they may "explain" it in terms of a story of its creation by an inferior or malevolent god; if they perceive the world as essentially good and themselves as at home in it, the story will be of its creation by the supreme or benevolent god.[6] We may suggest that the

[6]Discussion of the nature and function of myth in the Bible may be found in B.S. Childs, *Myth and Reality in the Old Testament,* London, 1960; G.B. Caird, *The Language and Imagery of the Bible,* London, 1980, chapter 13; and J.D.G. Dunn, "Demythologizing—the Problem of Myth in the New Testament," in I.H. Marshall, ed., *New Testament Interpretation,* Exeter, 1977.

two sections of the Apocalypse are not progressive from what precedes them, but relate back as an interpretation of it. In stage (6) we are shown through the use of powerful symbolism which is so characteristic of apocalyptic what the author believes to be the nature of the present time, why it should be seen as the time before the end, and the current struggle in its true dimensions. Similarly when the symbols recur after the judgment cycle, the nature and the reason for the judgment are being expounded: 16:19 refers to the fall of the great city; chapter 17 presents "Babylon" in her true colours to explain the inevitability of her fate. To much of this we shall return, as also to suggest an explanation for the two parts of the vision of the future: the millennial kingdom (stage 9) and the new heaven and earth (stage 10).

One way of approaching a document, then, is by considering its genre and structure; another is through examination of its historical setting and initial reference. For some schools of modern literary criticism there is between the two a great gulf fixed, but in the context of apocalyptic the distinction is blurred, since one characteristic of the genre is precisely its concern with "situation"; the conviction that the time for which it is written is the time of the final crisis and divine intervention. So we may ask where this conviction comes from, whether it is simply a dogmatic assertion or related to reflection upon particular circumstances.

It is clear that the seer of the Apocalypse associated the divine intervention which he expected imminently with other imminent events. He expected the Christian churches to suffer martyrdom on a large scale. In his vision, the martyrs seen under the heavenly altar are told to wait until the number of their brethren to be killed should be complete (6:11); the great multitude of 7:14 are those who have come out of the great "tribulation"; in 11:7-9 God's two witnesses are killed in the great city; there are those who "loved not their lives even unto death" (12:11); the blood of the saints and prophets has been shed (16:6); the great harlot is drunk with the blood of saints and martyrs (17:6); the blood of prophets and saints is found in Babylon (18:24); but God is said to avenge the blood of his servants (19:2), and in the millennial kingdom thrones are given to those who had been beheaded for their testimony (20:4). It is equally clear where he expected this massive attack to come from. It is the beast who makes war on the saints (13:7), and he has seven heads which are interpreted as "seven hills" (13:1, 17:9); unmistakably the famous seven hills of Rome. Similarly the great harlot is "the great city which has dominion over the kings of the earth" (17:18). What is expected is an attack upon the Christian churches by the Roman state.

What is not clear is why the seer should expect such an attack. It does not seem that it has yet been launched. Certainly something has already happened: a man called Antipas has been killed in Pergamum (2:13), and John himself, who regards himself as a sharer in tribulation and endurance, was on the island of Patmos off the coast of Asia Minor "on account of the word of God and the testimony of Jesus" (1:9). Early tradition has it that he was there as a legal penalty, because he had been banished there; islands, as providing natural confines, were popular places of banishment under Roman administration.[7] But, even accepting this, it does not amount to much to explain the author's predictions and his warnings to the churches about "what you are about to suffer" (2:10, to Pergamum) and "the hour of trial which is coming" (3:10, to Philadelphia).

---

[7] Tertullian writes that John was *in insulam relegatur* (*De praescriptione haereticorum* 36). There were three forms of banishment that might be imposed under the Roman legal system: (a) to penal servitude in quarries or mines, imposed only on those of low rank, like the slave pope Callistus who was sent to the mines of Sardinia ca. A.D. 190; (b) *deportatio*, the exiling with deprivation of civil rights and property of those of high rank, imposed by the Emperor, as Herod Antipas was banished by Caligula in A.D. 39; and (c) *relegatio*, compulsory residence in a specified area, under pain of death, imposed on persons of some standing by the provincial governor. The third seems the most probable for John and would correspond to the language of Tertullian the lawyer. There is no evidence, literary or archaeological, that Patmos was used as a "penal settlement" (so Charles and others, citing Pliny, *Naturalis Historia* IV.12.23,69, which says no such thing), but its small area and rocky terrain make it a suitable choice for a place of confinement. Patmos was within the jurisdiction of the city of Miletus and thus of the provincial governor of Asia, and from John's concern with the churches in seven cities in Asia it seems likely that it was from there that he was banished. For a contrary view, that he was banished from Palestine, see J.N. Sanders, "St. John on Patmos," *New Testament Studies* 9 (1962-63), pp. 75-85.

The author's expectation may therefore come not so much from what has actually happened already, but from "the nature of the beast": the way the Roman state was presenting itself, or the way that he perceived it. It is characteristic of the beast in his vision that it demands and is given worship (13:4), and that under penalty of death (13:15). This worship is enforced by a second beast which "rose out of the earth," and which makes an image of the first (13:11-15). Those who take part in the worship receive the mark of the name or number of the beast, which is "a human number" (13:18; other references to the worship of the beast are found in 14:9, 11; 16:2; 19:20 and 20:4).

The obvious interpretation of this emphasis upon a requirement to worship the beast is that the seer's expectation of conflict with Rome is related to the state cult, and especially (because the number of the beast is "a human number" or "the number of a man") the imperial cult. Reverence for the ruler as sacred, indeed divine, was an ancient tradition for the peoples of the eastern Mediterranean kingdoms and was readily transferred by them to their western conquerors, first Hellenistic, with Alexander the Great and his successors, then Roman. These latter rulers may have accepted their cult with reserve and even cynicism (though no doubt also as politically useful),[8] but it always remained very popular and vigorously supported in the province of Asia, where cities vied with each other to be the centre of the cult for that province, and thus to bear the title "Temple Warden." Three of the cities of John's seven churches, Ephesus, Smyrna and Pergamum, held the title at various times in the Julio-Claudian period; and in other ways his cities had a notable record of participation: Smyrna set up a temple to "Tiberius, Livia and the Holy Senate": Pergamum had one to

---

[8]Augustus and Tiberius did not permit the dedication of temples to themselves alone in their lifetimes, but rather to the "genius" of the emperor or to him alongside "holy Roma." Deification of the emperor happened after his death; hence the quip of the dying soldier-emperor Vespasian, "I think I'm becoming a god" (Suetonius, *De Vita Caesarum,* Vespasian 23). The cult is ruthlessly satirized by the Roman intellectual Seneca, in his account of the *Apocolocyntosis,* the "pumpkinification" of Claudius, with its picture of the emperor limping into heaven to the scandal of the other gods (a translation may be found as an appendix to Robert Graves, *Claudius the God,* London, 1954).

"Augustus and Roma"; Ephesus was where the representatives of Asia had declared Julius Caesar to be "god manifest"; while Sardis, Philadelphia and Laodicea supply evidence for the cult's continuing into the second century under Trajan, Hadrian and their successors. If there was an emperor who in fact welcomed or encouraged acknowledgment of his deity, we would expect the cities of Asia to take this up with alacrity. Such emperors were Gaius (Caligula), Nero and Domitian.[9]

The earliest tradition about the Apocalypse is that it was written under Domitian, who reigned from A.D. 81–96,[10] and this is consistent with evidence about Domitian. That he encouraged homage to himself as divine is agreed by those like Suetonius and Juvenal who bitterly attacked him after his death, and reflected in the work of the court poets Martial and Statius who flattered him during his life; and in particular he adopted the title *Dominus et Deus*, so that his orders were conveyed in the form "Our Lord and God instruct you to do this!" (Suetonius, *Vita Caes.*, Domitian 13).[11] He also reintroduced the dreaded trials for *maiestas*, treason, a crime under which much could be, and was, subsumed; notably, once a ruler claimed divinity, any attack on his dignity could be construed as treason, and "Domitian did not hesitate to punish as *laesa maiestas* offences in either word or deed against his person".[12] Furthermore, at some point during his reign there began the building, in the centre of Ephesus, of an enormous temple to Domitian the living god. It contained a colossal statue of the

[9]Accounts of the state or imperial cult may be found in *The Oxford Classical Dictionary*, Oxford, 1949, under "Ruler Cult" by M. Hammond; C.N. Cochrane, *Christianity and Classical Culture,* Oxford, 1940, chapters III and IV; and, in particular for the cult in the province of Asia, J. Ferguson, *The Religions of the Roman Empire,* London, 1970, chapter VI.

[10]Irenaeus, *Adversus Haereses,* V.30.3, quoted and enlarged on by Eusebius, *H.E.* III.18; also Clement of Alexandria, *Quis Dives Salvetur?* 42.

[11]For Domitian's adoption of the title , see K. Scott, *The Imperial Cult under the Flavians,* Stuttgart-Berlin, 1936, reprinted New York 1975, chapter VIII. Scott argues that the title was derived from the East.

[12]*Ibid.,* p. 129.

divine emperor (from the fragments it is calculated to have been five metres high if he were seated and seven if he were standing) and it was this building achievement that won for Ephesus that coveted title "temple warden".[13] It is easy to imagine the impact this enterprise would have upon an Asian Christian: as a preparation for the worship of a man as "Our Lord", the most characteristic Christian title for Jesus, it would seem the ultimate blasphemy. He would find himself alienated from his enthusiastic fellow-citizens, maybe already attracting their hostility, and open to accusations of treason.

There are, inevitably, difficulties in the way of accepting the dating of the Apocalypse under Domitian. He is entrenched in Christian tradition as the second persecutor of the Church, "a second Nero for cruelty",[14] but, unlike the persecution of Nero, this is not confirmed by non-Christian sources whose accounts read more like a palace purge of those too near the emperor for his sense of safety. [15] However, we do not have to suppose an attack launched by Domitian himself, and, in any event, the Apocalypse speaks rather of the expectation than the experience of persecution. Even if Domitian himself did not persecute Christians, his reign and the especial conditions of Asia Minor provided the circumstances in which they may very well have come under attack, or expected to, at the initiative of their fellow-citizens. Further difficulties are presented within the Apocalypse itself, in the symbolic references to the number-name of the beast which is the number of a man (13:18) and to the seven heads of the beast which are seven hills and also seven

---

[13]For a description of the Domitian temple at Ephesus, see Scott, *op. cit.,* p. 96f., and E. Akurgal, *Ancient Civilizations and Ruins of Turkey,* 2nd edn. Istanbul, 1970, pp. 166, 168.

[14]Tertullian, *Apologeticum* 5; Eusebius's account in *H.E.* III.17-20.7 is drawn from sources including Irenaeus, Tertullian and the Apocalypse itself.

[15]Suetonius, *Vita Caes.,* Domitian 15; Dio Cassius, *Epitome* LXVII.14. Dio's reference to accusations of "atheism" and "Jewish customs" could be understood in terms of Christianity, but this is neither explicit nor a necessary interpretation of them.

kings (17:9-10). Neither of these cryptograms can be immediately cracked to yield Domitian as its solution, but neither presents an insuperable problem,[16] and overall the traditional dating continues to make good sense. [17]

To draw together the threads of this introduction, then, we shall approach the study of the Apocalypse on the assumption that it belongs to the literary genre of apocalyptic, and that it was written to address the situation in which the author found himself in the province of Asia in the reign of the emperor Domitian. Nothing of this should, however, be taken to prejudge its character as prophecy. Every word of prophecy, as every work of literature, is initially given in a form and in a setting; but as it is true of great literature that it will transcend both form and setting (and we shall argue that the vision of John is not controlled and determined by its apocalyptic form), so that may also be true of prophecy.

[16]For a discussion of the number of the beast, see pp. 47-51, and for the seven kings, see note 14 to that discussion on p. 51.

[17]For a contrary view, dating the Apocalypse in A.D. 68, see C. Rowland, *The Open Heaven,* pp. 403-413.

2

"I Saw a Lamb"

Having outlined the principles upon which we will approach the Apocalypse, we may now embark upon the mainstream of our study of it. The aim is to show that the book's great central image of Christ as the Lamb serves to control and interpret other major themes. The Lamb who is the lamp of the holy city sheds light on some and casts others into shadow; we shall look at image and at mirror-image, at imitation and at parody.

We begin not with the image of the Lamb itself, but with the first image of Christ in the Apocalypse, that of him as "one like a son of man" in 1:12-18. The image is a composite one, woven from several threads which we shall have to unpick and identify in order to appreciate its total effect. We have not far to go to discover its initial source: the phrase "one like a son of man" comes straight from Dan. 7:13, where it denotes a figure who comes with the clouds of heaven into the presence of God, the "Ancient of Days," to be given dominion by him. (Chapter 7 of Daniel is widely drawn on elsewhere in the Apocalypse, as we shall see; the connection between these two passages is neither isolated nor artificial.) There is room to debate the identity of Daniel's "son of man" in its original context, and the meaning of the phrase when it is used, as it characteristically is, by Jesus in the gospels; but it is clear that by the end of the first century A.D. the passage was understood to be about the Messiah,

God's appointed agent in the salvation of his people.[1] It is so understood by the author of 2 Esdras (4 Ezra), who draws on it in chapter 13, especially vv. 3-5, 32, and who may be a contemporary of the author of the Apocalypse; and in that section of the book of Enoch known as the "Similitudes" (1 Enoch 37-71, especially 46:1-3).

The "son of man" of the Apocalypse, then, recalls the figure of Daniel 7; he also recalls another figure from Daniel, the "man" of 10:5-6. Both are clothed in linen, girded with gold, with eyes like fire, feet like brass and a voice like "a multitude" (Dan. 10:6, Rev. 1:15, "the sound of many waters"). This "man" figure is identified in Daniel 10 as the champion of Israel, engaged in battle with the "princes" of Persia and Greece. He is thus engaged on the heavenly level of apocalyptic, but he is not Israel's "angel champion": that is, Michael, who fights on his side (10:13, 20-21). Most probably he is the Messiah, here conceived of as a heavenly figure rather than an earthly king, and John's association of this figure with the "son of man" of Daniel 7 (whether or not it is original to him) shows that he understood the latter also unambiguously as a messianic image.

Initially, then, we are presented with an image of Christ as the Messiah; but there is more to the total image than that. This son of man has hair "white as white wool, white as snow", and in this attribute he is reminiscent rather of Daniel's "one that was ancient of days" (Dan. 7:9). Not much should be made of this by

---

[1]The primary function of the phrase in Daniel 7 is as a symbol for righteous Israel, "the saints of the Most High" of 7:18, as the four beasts of the vision symbolize oppressive kings or kingdoms (7:17, 23). But the literature on the origins and associations of the term in general is immense, because, as it is almost exclusively used in the gospels by Jesus and most often in clear reference to himself, it could serve as a vital key to understanding how he interpreted his own rôle and identity. A guide to the debate may be found in I.H. Marshall, "The Son of Man Sayings in Recent Discussion", *N.T.S.* 12 (1965-66), 327-51, and a further contribution is made by B. Lindars, *Jesus, Son of Man,* London, 1983.

itself, since in the Septuagint (the Greek translation of the Bible made by the Jews in the Diaspora; and the form in which John read his Bible) the distinction between the two figures is blurred, with the son of man said to be "like one ancient of days" (Dan. 7:13). However, John's figure goes on to identify himself: "I am the first and the last, and the living one" (1:17-18a). This is immediately reminiscent of the self-revelation of God in the prophecy of second Isaiah: "I, the Lord, the first, and with the last; I am He" (Isa. 41:4, RSV translation of the Hebrew text; the Septuagint text gives: "I God am first and I am what is to come"); "I am He, I am the first and I am the last" (48:12, cf. also 44:6). It is also reminiscent of the Septuagint rendering of God's explanation to Moses of his divine name, and so the revelation of his identify as "I am he who is" (Exod. 3:14, Septuagint).[2] That we are right to catch in the self-revelation of John's Christ allusions to the self-revelation of God is confirmed by the fact that John uses the same language in other contexts expressly for God; the Lord God who in 1:8 declares himself to be "the Alpha and the Omega" is the one "who is and who was and who is to come" (for Christ as also "Alpha and Omega," see the concluding declarations of the Apocalypse, 22:13); and he is worshipped in those terms by the four living creatures of the vision of heaven (4:8). Also in the worship of heaven, God is acclaimed as "who art and who wast" (11:17, 16:5) and as the one "who lives for ever and ever" (4:9, cf. 15:7). The second element in John's image of Christ as the son of man is that he is to be understood in terms of the character of God.

However, there is an important distinction between the two. Although in being "first, last and living", the son of man is seen as like God, he has this character because "I died, and behold I am alive for evermore" (1:18b). He is a figure who belongs to

---

[2]The origins and meaning of the Hebrew divine name *Yahweh* (rendered traditionally in English as "Jehovah") are notoriously obscure. The explanation of it in the Hebrew text of Exodus connects the name with the verb *hayah,* to be, though even there the force of the connection is not clear, as is apparent from the different translations suggested in the RSV: "I am who I am" or "I am what I am" or "I will be what I will be". The LXX translation is an interpretation in abstract, metaphysical terms more at home in Greek thought.

past, to present and to future in virtue of his death and resurrection to life. There are then three dimensions to this first image of Christ in the Apocalypse: the initial messianic image is expanded first in terms of the language of God and secondly in relation to "the facts of Jesus", the central pattern of the Christian kerygma.

This threefold effect may again be observed when we turn to the second image of Christ in the book, that of him as the Lamb. The Lamb first appears in 5:5-7, in the vision of heaven; then with the heavenly army in 14:1; and further in reference to his marriage in 19:7,9 and his bride in 21:9. These, together with many passing references, make it the most frequently used term for Christ, and it is congruously developed with more complexity. As before, the image draws initially upon messianic tradition. In 5:5 the seer is directed to expect "the Lion of the tribe of Judah, the Root of David", and the language derives from two passages which were conventionally given a messianic interpretation: the description of Judah in the "Blessing of Jacob" as "a lion's whelp" and as the one from whom "the scepter shall not depart" (Gen. 49:9-12); and Isaiah's prophecy of "a shoot from the stump of Jesse", David's father, "a branch . . . out of his roots", who will bear the Lord's spirit and be a righteous ruler (Isa. 11:1-5). It is consistent with this introduction of him in messianic terms that the Lamb bears seven horns (5:6): he is a young ram, endowed with power and strength; as in 14:1 he is a warrior, leading his army in holy war.

In view of these latter characteristics of John's Lamb it is sometimes argued that the term "lamb" was itself already established as a messianic image or title; but the evidence for this is very shaky. In the Testaments of the Twelve Patriarchs Test. Joseph 19:8 speaks of a lamb-messiah, but as he is further described as "born of a virgin", this is almost certainly a Christian interpolation in the course of textual transmission; if indeed the Testaments are not originally a Christian composition. In 1 Enoch 85-90 we have a survey of the history of Israel from Adam to the expected Messiah, using animal imagery: until the Exodus the story is of "bulls", thereafter of the vicissitudes of God's sheep. Periodically a lamb is selected to become a ram and lead the flock: thus Saul and David (1 Enoch 89:42-48), and the Maccabees (90:9-10). However, when we come to the Messiah in 90:37-38 the text is tantalizingly corrupt. He is introduced as a white bull, like Adam, but seems then to become something else: according to the text as it stands, "a word"; a reading so obviously obscure that it has been emended by some scholars, notably the great editor of the Pseudepigrapha, R.H. Charles, to read "a lamb."This reading is probably also wrong, and Charles's suggestion is not adopted by more recent editors and translators.[3] The most we can say is that the familiar image of the people of God as his flock (e.g. Ps. 95:7; Is. 40:11; Jer. 23:2-4; Ezek. 34:2-16) could well produce the image of their leader as a ram, but there is no evidence that this development had in fact been made in relation to the Messiah. Most probably the identification of his central figure as "the Lamb" is John's own addition to the messianic language which he has so far echoed. He "hears" the familiar titles in 5:5; in 5:6 he "sees" something new: a Lamb. This transition from hearing to seeing as from the familiar to the new is a pattern which we shall observe elsewhere in his vision.

All this aside, however, the second image of Christ begins in messianic terms: the introduction of the lion of Judah, the root of David. The Lamb who is thus introduced, though, has "seven eyes, which are the seven spirits of God sent out into all the earth" (5:6). It is possible to understand this as reflecting the endowment of the Messiah with the seven-fold spirit, "the Spirit of the Lord shall rest upon him, the spirit of wisdom and understanding, the spirit of counsel and might, the spirit of knowledge and the fear of the Lord" (Isa. 11:2); but a more probable source for the image is Zechariah 4, another chapter

---

[3]The reading is anyway at odds with the context of Enoch's parable, in which the messianic age is a return to the righteousness of the patriarchal, "white bull", period, not subsequent "sheeplike" weakness! The emendation is not adopted by M.A. Knibb in his edition of the text, *The Ethiopic Book of Enoch,* vol. 2(Oxford, 1978), nor does it appear in the recent editions of J. Charlesworth, *The Old Testament Pseudepigrapha,* vol. 1, New York, 1983, or H.F.D. Sparks, *The Apocryphal Old Testament,* Oxford, 1984. It still finds a defender, though, in B. Lindars, "A Bull, a Lamb and a Word: 1 Enoch 90:38", *N.T.S.* 22 (1975-76), 483-86.

widely influential on the language of the Apocalypse. There the seven "eyes" which "range through the whole earth" (4:10) are expressly "the eyes of the Lord"; once again the messianic language is extended in terms of the language or imagery of God. It is consistent with this detail in the opening image that the Lamb later appears as the bridegroom of the new Jerusalem (19:7, 9 and 21:9), as Yahweh is familiarly presented as the bridegroom or husband of Israel (for example, Isa. 54:5f.; Ezek, 16:8ff.; Hos. 2:14-20).

More dramatically, though, John sees his Lamb "standing, as though it had been slain" (5:6); a violent wrenching of the visual image into one that is anything but naturalistic, but which seems to bring him within the framework of distinctively Christian imagery: that of Christ as the sacrificial lamb. Thus, for the author of 1 Peter, Christ is "like ... a lamb without blemish or spot" whose blood provides a ransom (1 Pet. 1:19); in the Fourth Gospel he is "the Lamb of God, who takes away the sin of the world" (Jn. 1:29,36), and he dies on the day that the passover lambs are sacrificed, himself fulfilling the regulation that, like them, "not a bone of him shall be broken" (19:6; cf. Exod. 12:46); and for Paul too "Christ, our paschal lamb, has been sacrificed" (1 Cor. 5:7). It may well be that in his picture of Christ as the slain Lamb John is making use of an image now familiar in Christian interpretation of his death, but two qualifications should be made before the conclusion is simply drawn. First, John's word for "Lamb" is the Greek *arnion,* which he uses consistently and invariably in contrast to the regular use of *amnos* by other New Testament authors and in the Septuagint. It is a small linguistic point of which not much should be made, but if John is simply echoing a commonplace image we might expect him to do so in the common language.[4] Secondly, John's

---

[4]The only other use of *arnion* in the NT is Jn. 21:15, "Feed my lambs", in the chapter often regarded as an appendix to the Fourth Gospel by a later editor; upon such a slender thread a theory of authorship might be hung!

Lamb stands *hōs esphagemnon,* "as if it had been slaughtered." The verb used, *sphazō,* is not the usual word for sacrificial killing (which would be *thuō*); though it is occasionally used in that sense in the Septuagint. It is most commonly used of the butchery of animals, as it is in Isaiah's image of God's servant as "like a lamb that is led to the slaughter" (Isa. 53:7: the image is clearly drawn from the abbatoir or the farm rather than the temple, as the conjunction with the image of "a sheep before its shearers" makes clear); or of the violent killing of men, as in war in Rev. 6:4, and significantly, in the violent deaths of Christian martyrs in Rev. 6:9, 18:24. In general, the language of salvation in the Apocalypse is not characteristically the language of sacrifice and of expiation of sins (we shall turn later to examine what are its distinctive terms); here, for example, the Lamb is associated not with the altar in heaven but with the throne (5:6-7), and in 1:5 and 5:9 his blood is the means of freedom and of purchase rather than of atonement.

It may be, then, that when the author of the Apocalypse identifies Christ as "the Lamb", he is using an image that had already become familiar in Christian, and especially in Johannine, circles; but the terms in which he expresses it are his own. He does not use the image with the unambiguously sacrificial connotations of the gospel of John and the first epistle of Peter, but yet because his lamb is the *slaughtered* Lamb the image is unequivocally related to the fact of the death of Jesus, and because that slaughtered Lamb is "standing", it is related also to his resurrection and life. Again, then, the image of Christ has three dimensions to it: the traditional imagery of the Messiah is extended first in terms of the imagery of God, and secondly in terms of the facts of Jesus.

As the image of the Lamb is to provide our key to unlocking other themes in the Apocalypse, we might now conclude our brief survey of the imagery of Christ in the vision; but there remains a third image, and since it is perhaps the most problematical, it should not be left without some comment. It is that of the rider on the white horse of 19:11-16. He is not, of course, the horseman who appears on his white steed at the opening of the first seal and the beginning of the cycle of preliminary woe

(6:2), though they have traits in common in that both are crowned and go to conquer. This second rider is clearly to be seen in the light of the preceding images of Christ: his flaming eyes and the sword from his mouth identify him as the one like a son of man (19:12, 15; cf. 1:14, 16); and the pattern of transition from what is heard to what is seen, which we observed in the image of the Lamb, recurs here, for voices alert the seer to expect the marriage of the Lamb (19:6-8), and what he then sees is the rider. The identity of the rider with the Lamb is affirmed in the fact that the "name" inscribed on the rider's robe and thigh, "King of kings and Lord of lords" (19:16), has already been the title of the Lamb (17:14).

Unambiguously, then, the image of the rider is an image of Christ; and equally obviously it is in the first place a messianic image. The conception of the Messiah as conquering warrior and righteous judge is conventional enough, and given a classic expression about a century before the Apocalypse in the Psalms of Solomon 17:23-51 ("Behold, O Lord, and raise up unto them their king, the son of David.... And gird him with strength, that he may shatter unrighteous rulers"). Specifically, in ruling the nations "with a rod of iron" (19:15) he performs the function of God's anointed, his son, in Psalm 2:9 (also echoed in Ps. Sol. 17:5); and in smiting them with the sword from his mouth also that of the Davidic king of Isaiah 11:4 (who will "smite the earth with the rod of his mouth"; cf. Ps. Sol. 17:10, 45). However, the title that the rider and the Lamb bear, "King of kings and Lord of lords" (19:16, 17:14), is not so much a messianic title as one which echoes the Deuteronomic description of God as "God of gods and Lord of lords" (Deut. 10:17), and Nebuchadnezzar's admission to Daniel that "Truly, your God is God of gods and Lord of kings" (Dan 2:47). The rider is also the one who "will tread the wine press of the fury of the wrath of God the Almighty" (19:15b); and now the source of the language is in the image of God as the vintager who has trodden the wine press alone, as the executioner of his wrath (Isa. 63:1-6). The second dimension in the image of the rider is that he has divine attributes and performs divine functions. The outstanding question is whether the image of Christ as the rider has that third dimension which we observed in the other two Christ images: their clear

relation to the tradition of the death and resurrection of Jesus.
The rider wears a robe "dipped in blood" (19:13)[5]; and commentators, like the sleuths of detective fiction, enquire "Whose
blood?". An obvious answer is that the blood is the rider's own
blood: the blood of the Lamb. We have already noted one
earlier reference to the blood of the Lamb, as the means of
redemption, in 5:9; in 7:14 the Lamb's followers have made their
robes white with it, and in 12:11 it is the means of victory. It
might seem appropriate that the conquering figure of the rider
should bear on his robe too the marks of victory, and Morris[6]
and Sweet[7] in their commentaries find the reference unmistakable. If it is so, then the rider as an image of Christ is also
unambiguously the Jesus of the cross. However, as we have
seen, the clearest allusion in the image is to the figure of Isaiah
63, who has stained his garments in treading the wine press, in
wrath and in the conquest of his enemies. That emphasis on
"wrath" (Isa. 63:3, 6) is taken up in the Apocalypse's reference
also to "the wine press of the fury of the wrath of God the
Almighty" (19:15; cf. 14:20). For R.H. Charles, the marks of
conquest which the rider bears are those of the blood of his
enemies.[8] Yet another point of reference is taken up by G.B.
Caird, who notes that in 14:20 the wine press is trodden "outside
the city", a detail strongly evocative of the crucifixion of Jesus
and so of his followers' commitment to it (cf. Heb. 13:12-13,
Jesus suffered "outside the gate ... therefore let us go forth to
him outside the camp"); and also that the imagery of wine is
associated with the blood not of Christ but of the martyrs. In
16:19 Babylon is given by God the cup of wrath, but in 17:6 the

---

[5]"Dipped", *bebammenon* from the verb *baptō*, is the reading with the best manuscript
support; variant readings using the verbs *rainō* and *rantizō* which describe the robe as
"sprinkled" with blood, a description with connotations of sacrifice (cf. Exod. 24:6-8; 1
Pet. 1:2, 19), are likely to be scribal "improvements" (so also B. Metzger, *A Textual
Commentary on the Greek New Testament,* New York, 1971, p. 763).

[6]L. Morris, *Revelation,* Tyndale New Testament Commentary, Leicester, 1971, p. 230.

[7]J. Sweet, *Revelation,* SCM Pelican Commentary, London, 1979, p. 283.

[8]R.H. Charles, *The Revelation of St. John,* International Critical Commentary, vol. 2,
Edinburgh, 1920, p. 133.

"wine" with which the harlot is drunk is the blood of saints and martyrs. For Caird, then, the image of the rider with his blood-stained robe is certainly an image of divine judgment, but that judgment is given in the death of the martyrs.[9]

All this somewhat tortuous discussion may be said to be the result of isolating one detail in the image and taking it literally. The "robe dipped in blood" which the rider wears is part of his character as the vintager of Isaiah 63, and the total image in both passages is a coherent one: he who treads the wine press dyes his garments with "the blood of the grape" (a familiar idiom found, for example, in Deut. 32:14, Ecclus. 39:26).[10] Moreover, there is another Old Testament figure who has his garments similarly stained: the "lion" Judah, who "washes his garments in wine and his vesture in blood of grapes" (Gen. 49:11). Now we know that the rider is the Lamb, and that the Lamb is the "Lion of the tribe of Judah" (5:5f.), so that it is not surprising to find the characteristic features of the latter recurring,[11] giving us as before an interplay of messianic and divine imagery.[12]

The main thrust of the image of the rider on the white horse is, then, to show the Christ-figure exercising the function of God; and in Revelation 19 as in Isaiah 63 that function is the execution of judgment and vengeance. If our third dimension,

---

[9]G.B. Caird, *The Revelation of St. John the Divine,* Black's New Testament Commentary, London, 1966, pp. 244-46.

[10]It is worth noting that the second half of Isa. 63:6, in which the reference is unambiguously and literally to the "lifeblood" of Yahweh's enemies, is absent from the Septuagint text as we know it, and in which John would have read it.

[11]In fact, in Gen. 49:11 Judah is himself a rider, "binding his foal to the vine and his ass's colt to the choice vine", which would strengthen the suggested link with Rev. 19, if the parallel were not thought too fanciful!

[12]There is some evidence that Isa. 63:1-6 and Gen. 49:10-11 were associated with each other in Jewish exegesis, though it is not clear how early that link was established; references may be found in J. Bowker, *The Targums and Rabbinic Literature,* Cambridge, 1969, pp. 290f. The present argument, for the association of the two passages in the Apocalypse and its implications, is given in more detail in Sophie Laws, "The blood-stained horseman: Revelation 19:11-13", *Journal for the Study of the New Testament,* Supplement Series 3, 1980 (*Studia Biblica* 1978), pp. 245-48.

the clear relation of the Christ image to the facts of Jesus, is absent, it may seem that we have now lost sight of his redemptive function. Here it is important to remember the position of this third image in the structure of the book as we have earlier outlined it. The one like a son of man in chapter 1, our stage (1), is the present Christ among the churches; the Lamb of chapter 5, stage (3), is the exalted Christ present in heaven. In both cases, he is what he is now because of what he has done: he has died and risen, and this gives him "the keys of Death and Hades" and the authority "to take the scroll and to open its seals" (1:18, 5:9). In chapter 19, though, we are in stage (9), after the uninterrupted cycle of the bowls of wrath. Now the vision is of the future, of final judgment and victory and the end itself, and the function of Christ changes accordingly. We are not allowed to forget that he is the Lamb, going to his marriage, and he still has the attributes of the son of man, but his act of redemption is complete and now he is the judge. There is a change in the content and character of the Christ image, and some, like Luther, may find it too violent for that image still to be a "Christian" one, but it is not without parallel in the New Testament. In the epistle to the Hebrews, too, there is a contrast between the vision of Christ as now the great High Priest, who has made the effective sacrifice in his death and lives in heaven, giving confidence to "draw near to the throne of grace" (Heb. 4:14-16, 5:25-27); and the expectation of his second appearance "not to deal with sin", so that there is no prospect of any second chance of redemption, but only of judgment (9:28, 10:26f.).

One comment in conclusion: in analyzing the images as we have, we may have made their construction seem very deliberate and very cerebral, as if the author composed them with the aid of a concordance, and we should qualify this impression. It is always important to distinguish between intention and function, and between the genesis of an image and its impact. What we have been considering is the images as they are, and in their effect: how they serve to present Jesus Christ as the Messiah of expectation, but also in relation to God, and also again as the Jesus of cross and resurrection. Whether the images came to the author in the oil-burning of the study, or as his cultural heritage, or in the givenness of visionary experience, it is not our intention here to speculate: they could spring equally from the mind of the scholar, the soul of the poet, or the spirit of the prophet; or indeed from all three in one.

3

The Adversaries

After our far from comprehensive survey of the leading images of Christ in the Apocalypse, we now turn to consider the images of those whom the seer regards as the adversaries of Christ and his churches, and our method will be the same: to ask how the images are constructed, where they are derived from, and what is their impact. The most prominent of these images is, of course, that of the beast, who is described in 13:1-18 and 17:3, 7-13; in our stages (6) and (8), whose function is to interpret the situation in which the author finds himself and its, to him, inevitable consequences. We have already seen that the beast is presented in terms of Rome and her rulers, with his seven heads which are seven hills as well as seven kings (13:1, 17:9-10); and his ten horns which are "ten kings who ... give over their power and authority to the beast" (17:12-13) may readily be understood as puppet monarchs within the imperial sway. However, there is not just a simple, one-to-one equation: beast = Rome, for the image of the beast evokes ideas and memories of other empires. The ten-horned beast is also "like a leopard, its feet were like a bear's, and its mouth was like a lion's mouth" (13:2). He thus has the characteristics of the four beast-empires of the vision of Dan. 7:4-6 (the chapter we found influential in John's image of Christ as the "one like a son of man"): he is the lion, Babylon; the bear, Media; the leopard, Persia; and the ten-horned monster of Greece all rolled into one.[1] If the beast of the Apocalypse is Rome, he is Rome seen as the climax or consummation of the history of the wickedness of pagan empires.

The same point may be made about a second image, that of the harlot, found in 17:1-7, 15-18. She is also in the first place an image of Rome, for she is seated on the seven hills (17:9), and is identified as "the great city which has dominion over the kings of the earth" (17:18); and as the beast is seen to "make war on the saints" (13:7), so the harlot is "drunk with the blood of the saints" (17:6). Again, though, there is not the simple equation: the harlot who is the great city = Rome, for as the image of the beast evoked ideas of other empires, so this one recalls other cities. This debauched and promiscuous woman is named "Babylon" (17:4-5), and this echoes the characterization of Babylon, the captor of Jerusalem in 586 B.C. and instigator of her people's exile, as the virgin put to shame in Isaiah 47. In 18:9-19 the kings and merchants of the earth lament the great city, itemizing her wealth and the trade that flowed to her in terms strongly reminiscent of the lament for Tyre in Ezekiel 26-27 (especially 26:16-18). When the bodies of God's witnesses are left to lie in the streets of the great city, that city is called "Sodom and Egypt" (11:8), and is thus shown as the inheritor or the epitome of the wicked cities where God's people have been rejected or persecuted (for Egypt, see Exodus 1-2, 5-11: the oppression of Israel in Egypt before the exodus was an indelible part of her memory; for Sodom, Genesis 19:1-29, with its account of the attack on Lot and the two angels). The city of the Apocalypse is also "where their Lord was crucified" (11:8), a clause often regarded as a gloss or an interpolation into the text,

---

[1]The identification of the four kings, or kingdoms, of Daniel 7 is drawn from analogy with the allegory of the dream of Nebuchadnezzar as four kingdoms in Dan. 2:31-45, where the first kingdom is Babylon, Nebuchadnezzar's own; and the vision of the two-horned ram and the he-goat in Dan. 8:3-26, which supplies the further sequence of Media, Persia and Greece. This latter vision also indicates that the "Greece" of the situation of the book of Daniel is the Hellenistic kingdom of Seleucid Syria, which, under Antiochus IV Epiphanes, was perceived as the persecutor of God's people.

though in fact it seems quite consistent that for a Christian author Jerusalem, as the place of Jesus' unjust execution, must join the tradition of wicked cities. The images of the beast and the harlot, then, do not just identify the enemy but interpret it; they do not simply point to Rome as the great adversary but indicate her character and rôle as such.

There is, though, more to the picture than this. As the images of Christ as the Messiah had an added dimension in terms of the language of God, so the image of the beast is filled out in terms of the further image of the dragon, found first in 12:3-17. Thus it is the dragon who "gave his power and throne and great authority" to the beast (13:2) so that the beast is worshipped with the dragon (13:4), and the second beast who is the lackey of the first is said to "speak like a dragon" (13:11). As the beast has seven heads and ten horns (13:1), so had the dragon before him (12:3); and as the dragon is "red" (12:3), so the beast is "scarlet" (17:4).[2] Quite apart from all his other characteristics, the beast also looks like a dragon; and the vision further strains the imagination!

The images of the beast and dragon interchange and interact; but while the beast is an adversary on earth, the dragon is a "portent ... in heaven" (12:3), and involved in "war ... in heaven" (12:9). It may well be that, as is often suggested, the image has links with astrology, with this dragon in the heavens as the constellation Scorpio, but its most immediate and important origin is in creation mythology. Many religions of the ancient Near East had as their creation myth a story of the battle between the creator god and a chaos monster: thus the religions of Canaan, Egypt and especially Babylon, whose story of the battle between the god Marduk and the monster Tiamat is given

---

[2]The words are different in Greek, *purros,* fiery red, and *kokkinos,* scarlet, respectively; so this is not a point to be pressed.

classic expression in the *Enûma Elish*.[3] Israel did not adopt this myth, though she may well have taken it over, as it were, "demythologized", for both the *Enûma Elish* and Genesis 1:2 refer to a watery chaos before creation, and the Hebrew word for the great "deep", *tĕhôm,* is etymologically related to "Tiamat". (The beast comes out of "the sea" in Rev. 13:1, recalling Israel's creation myth in its normative biblical form.)

Yet although a battle between God and a chaos monster is no part of the story of creation in Genesis 1 and 2, it is clear from other parts of the Old Testament that the myth was familiar in Israel and used in various ways. It is "historicized", or used to interpret history, in Ezek. 32:2-8, where Pharaoh of Egypt is depicted as "a dragon in the seas" (v.2), to be slaughtered by God. Egypt is also Rahab the dragon (the origins and meaning of the name are obscure, but the reference is clear) in Isaiah 30:7, and 51:9-10, where the imagery of the conquest of the dragon and subduing of the sea is used of the historical event of the Exodus, God's "creation" of Israel. The language of the myth also gives expression to eschatological hope in Isa. 27:1: "In that day the Lord ... will punish Leviathan the fleeing serpent, Leviathan the twisting serpent, and he will slay the dragon that is in the sea"; the new age will be a new creation.

Further, and very strikingly, the language of the myth is kept alive, apparently without any such reinterpretation or domestication in terms of Israel's normative tradition, in the Psalms, where Yahweh is celebrated as the one who "didst divide the sea by thy might ... didst break the heads of the dragons on the waters ... didst crush the heads of Leviathan" (Ps. 74:13-14), and who "dost rule the raging of the sea ... didst crush Rahab like a carcass" (Ps. 89:9-10); and in Job, where "by his power he stilled the sea; by his understanding he smote Rahab ... his

[3] A translation of the *Enûma Elish* may be found in J.B. Pritchard, *Ancient Near Eastern Texts Relating to the Old Testament,* 3rd. edition, Princeton, 1969, pp. 60-72; and, together with other related Babylonian creation stories and a valuable discussion of Old Testament parallels, in A. Heidel, *The Babylonian Genesis,* 2nd. edition, Chicago, 1953 (though Heidel discusses whether Tiamat should be identified as a goddess rather than a dragon). A recent, exhaustive discussion of the dragon myth is provided by John Day, *God's Conflict with the Dragon and the Sea,* Cambridge, 1985.

hand pierced the fleeing serpent" (Job 26:12-13), and "beneath him bowed the helpers of Rahab" (9:13).[4] It is clear that, even though the dragon myth was not the creation myth of Genesis, the connotations of that image would be familiar to anyone within the Old Testament tradition; and the dragon of the Apocalypse has further direct links with that tradition: he is also "that ancient serpent, who is called the Devil and Satan" (12:9; cf. 20:2); the serpent, the deceiver of the Fall myth of Gen. 3:1-15, and Satan the accuser and angelic adversary of Zech. 3:1, Job 1-2, 1 Chron. 21:1, and of intertestamental literature, for example, the Apocalypse of Moses 17.

The image of the beast as the adversary is thus related by John to the image of the dragon, and this produces the two dimensions of the apocalyptic genre and world-view, but the relationship makes a very considerable impact. The idea that human states or nations had heavenly guardians and authorities is not extraordinary: Deuteronomy 32:8-9 in the Septuagint describes God as fixing the number of the nations "according to the number of the sons of God", the angels, while reserving Israel for himself,[5] and the same idea is found in Jubilees 15:31-32. Members of the heavenly council are held responsible or accountable for human affairs in Psalm 82 (the "gods, sons of the Most High" of vv. 1,6 would have come to be regarded as angels by monotheistic Judaism whatever their original character); Persia, Greece, and indeed Israel have, as we have seen, their angel "princes" in Dan. 10:20-21 and 12:1. The idea

[4]It is relevant to note that, as is reflected in Ps. 74:14, the dragon of the myth was traditionally a many-headed monster: Lotan, the dragon of Canaanite mythology, was seven-headed (Ras Shamra Tablet I AB; Pritchard, *op. cit.* p. 138). The seven heads of the dragon of the Apocalypse are integral to the image, and the beast has seven heads because he is the dragon's beast, and this should caution us against expecting an exact decoding of the riddle of 17:9-10 in terms of the Roman imperial succession. See further, note 14, p. 51.

[5]The Hebrew text as we have it describes the number of the nations as fixed "according to the number of the sons of Israel", but the RSV translation, unusually, prefers the Septuagint reading, regarding it as the translation of an earlier Hebrew version of the passage, and most scholars agree with this.

may play some part in Paul's notion of "principalities and powers": in Romans 13 he counsels "let every person be subject to the governing authorities. For there is no authority except from God, and those that exist have been instituted by God" (v. 1), and he goes on to talk of the administration of justice and the payment of taxes (vv. 4 and 6); but "authorities" ("powers" in KJV and RV) is a word used in relation to cosmic forces in Rom. 8:38f. and in Col. 1:15. These "guardians" of human government are subject to God's rebuke and to the exercise of his rule, but they are all, as it were, legitimate; they may be straying angels, but they are not outside the divine sphere. What John has done is to identify the guardian of Rome not with any angel, but with the great cosmic adversary of the creator God. (He transfers the notion of angelic guardians, in fact, from the nations to the churches, who each have their "angels" addressed in seven letters, 1:20, 2:1, etc.) His imagery of the adversaries is thus strongly dualistic, and its effect is to make an absolute divide between the churches and the Roman power.

Moreover, there is yet another dimension to the picture, for the image of the beast is dramatically related to the images of Christ. The Lamb of 5:6 stood "as though it had been slain", and the one like a son of man revealed that he is "the living one" who "died, and behold I am alive for evermore" (1:18); the beast has one head which "seemed to have a mortal wound, but its mortal wound was healed" (13:3),[6] and when these heads are seen as symbolic of kings, the eighth king who is the beast himself is one of the seven, fallen and returned (17:9-11). Whatever the derivation of this imagery in terms of contemporary reference, for instance to remembered rumours of the return of Nero,[7] its immediate effect is to show the beast as a parody of the Lamb. This parody theme has other variations. The son of man is "the first and the last, and the living one" (1:17f.), as God "is . . . and was and . . . is to come' (1:8); the beast, in a series of distorted

---

[6]Literally, the head was seen "as if it had been slaughtered": the same participle, from the verb *sphazō*, is used as for the Lamb in 5:6.

[7]See n. 14, p. 51.

echoes, "was, and is not, and is to ascend" or "was and is not and is to come" (17:8), "was and is not ... and it goes to perdition" (17:11). The second beast which "spoke like a dragon" also had two horns "like a lamb" (13:11). The one hundred and forty-four thousand servants of God who are "sealed" in 7:3 appear in 14:1 as the warriors of the Lamb, sealed on the forehead with his name and his Father's; in 13:16 the adherents of the beast receive on their right hand or forehead the "mark" which is his name or number. The rider on the white horse, that third image of Christ, has a name "which no one knows but himself" (19:12), an apparently secret name which is, however, promptly revealed as "the Word of God" (19:13); and the beast, of course, has his mystery name (13:18), and bears "a blasphemous name" (13:1, cf. 17:3; the parody of "the word of God" by "blasphemy" is especially sharp). Finally, worship is addressed to the Lamb with God (for example, 5:13f., and we shall examine the significance of the language of this worship); and the beast is worshipped with the dragon (13:4; we have already noted the recurrent theme of the demand of the beast for worship, p. 20).

Once again we may consider the effect of this interaction of images, for it serves to explain and interpret the conflict which the seer expects between the churches and the Roman power. This coming crisis is not just another event in the stream of history, one more "damn thing". It is the climax of the whole history of the antagonism of nations, empires and cities towards God's people; it is a product and a reflection of the great cosmic divide between the creator God and the power of chaos; and now we see that its essence is a conflict about Christ, whose status and rôle the Roman power blasphemously claims and parodies: a conflict which we can readily see as provoked by the imperial cult in its manifestation under Domitian, the living man who required to be called "our Lord and God." The imagery gives an ideological or theological basis to the sense of alienation and threat from contemporary society, it enforces the need for Christian separation from that society, for sectarian boundaries; it is inevitable and necessary that one who accepts the claims of Christ should find himself set against the power of Rome, for he must stand for God against the dragon and for the truth of the Lamb against the parody of the beast. There is no room for compromise. The Apocalypse of John makes a very clear statement in the perennial debate on the relation of religion and political power.[8] It is a very far cry from Paul's positive acceptance of state authority as "instituted by God" (Rom. 13:1), and of those who exercise it as "ministers of God" (v. 6) even to the extent that their justice is to be seen as an execution of "the wrath of God" (vv. 4-5); from Peter's similar instruction to "be subject for the Lord's sake to every human institution", both the emperor and his delegates the governors (1 Pet. 2:13-14), and his juxtaposing of the commands to "fear God" and "honour the emperor" (v. 17); even from Jesus' perhaps more guarded and more limited ruling, "render to Caesar the things that are Caesar's, and to God the things that are God's" (Mk. 12:17 and parallels).

The variety of these attitudes should caution us against trying to define "the" Christian, or even "the" New Testament, view of the state. It is, of course, relevant in assessing them to note that the judgments are made in different contexts: not only might Paul the Roman citizen be expected to take a different view of the empire than John the exile (though Paul had had his taste of Roman jails, for example, Acts 16:22-39, 24:23, 27); but both Paul and Peter are concerned with Roman power experienced in the administration of justice, of which the empire was rightly proud and from which its citizens greatly benefited (although a Christian would always be mindful of the outcome of the trial of Jesus), while John is faced with that power's claiming legitimacy and loyalty in religious terms.[9] The variety of views is also, however, a reminder of the constant need for Christian scrutiny and assessment of human power structures, for as John's beast

---

[8] These lectures were given during the 1984 American presidential campaign, when the issue surfaced again as very much alive.

[9] Discussion of New Testament attitudes to the state, including its cosmic dimension, may be found in O. Cullmann, *The State in the New Testament,* London, 1957; G.B. Caird, *Principalities and Powers,* Oxford, 1956; and C.D. Morrison, *The Powers That Be,* London, 1960.

is not simply Rome but evocative of other, past, powers hostile to God and his people, so the rôle of the beast may not be played out finally in Rome. Those who have read the Apocalypse as prophetic of Nazi Germany, Soviet Russia, the South Africa of apartheid, even the mediaeval papacy, may have been wrong to ignore the original historical setting of the vision and to suppose an exclusive one-to-one correspondence between image and event, but right to see that John's imagery can continue to have an interpretative value outside its initial circumstances. Whenever any human power structure seeks for itself absolute acceptance as a religious duty or finds in itself the sole means to human salvation, fulfilment or freedom, then it has about it the nature of the beast, and it is the duty of the people of God to dissociate themselves from it, even though that be at their peril.

We may pause briefly to speculate how John's own readers may have reacted to his uncompromising message: did they share his sense of alienation and danger and need a theological vision to enable them to cope with it, or did they regard the imperial cult as simply social custom, part of their world, and therefore need (to his mind) to be enlightened as to its true significance? The letters to the seven churches reveal that he had enemies, and that he felt the need for vigorous persuasion in many quarters. The church in Thyatira was under the influence of "the woman Jezebel, who calls herself a prophetess and is teaching and beguiling my servants to practice immorality and to eat food sacrificed to idols" (2:20), while in Pergamum there were some "who hold the teaching of Balaam, who taught Balak to put a stumbling block before the sons of Israel, that they might eat food sacrificed to idols and practice immorality" (2:14). The accusations of immorality and participation in idolatry are the same; the names are almost certainly pejorative epithets: the opponents are to be seen in the guise of Jezebel, the Phoenecian consort of King Ahab who used her power to encourage pagan religion in Israel (1 Kgs. 16:31-33, 18:18-19), and Balaam, the prophet hired by King Balak of Moab (Num. 22-28) who is also held responsible for Israel's worship of the god Baal of Peor (Num. 25:1-4, 31:16). Both names suggest an association of royal authority and disloyalty to God. It may be that at Thyatira and Pergamum express sanction had been given to participation in the imperial cult, by "teaching" or "prophecy", and John had to refute this; especially at Thyatira, for Pergamum had also the example of the martyrdom of Antipas "my faithful one, who was killed among you, where Satan dwells" (2:13, also "where Satan's throne is": Pergamum was, not entirely incidentally, the seat of the proconsul of the province of Asia).[10]

Also in Pergamum John warns that there are "some who hold the teaching of the Nicolaitans" (2:15), teaching which is rejected at Ephesus, where "you hate the works of the Nicolaitans, which I also hate"(2:6). There is no obvious way in which "Nicolaitan" can be seen as a symbolic name, and it is probable that it was the common, recognizable label for the group John characterizes as "Balaamite". Who the Nicolaitans were is unknown: tradition associates them (though for no obvious reason) with Nicolas the proselyte of Acts 6:5 (thus Clement of Alexandria, *Stromateis* III.4.25f., quoted by Eusebius, *H. E.* III.29.1-4; and Tertullian, *De Pudicitia* 19, *Adversus Marcionem* I.29, *De Praescriptione* 33). They appear as a gnostic sect in Irenaeus's great catalogue of heresies before and during his own time (*Adv. Haer.* I.26.3 and III.11.1), linked with the teaching of Cerinthus, the traditional opponent of the apostle John. If they were gnostics, they may well have regarded the imperial cult as a matter of this world order and therefore of indifference to the enlightened gnostic, who might participate in it without its touching his inner soul. However, Irenaeus's description of Nicolaitan teaching is almost wholly derived from the text of the Apocalypse, so he cannot be relied upon to give us any independent information with which to interpret the text.

John is also bitter against "those who say that they are Jews and are not, but are a synagogue of Satan" in Smyrna and Philadelphia (2:9, 3:9); this could be because Jews, from the

---

[10]A similar conclusion is reached by David Aune: "the conflict is not really over immorality and the eating of sacrificial meat alone, but over the stance toward cultural and religious accommodation which these practices symbolize", in "The Social Matrix of the Apocalypse of John", *Biblical Research* XXVI, 1981, p. 28.

security of their status as a legal religion, acted as *delatores,* bringing accusation against Christians before the Roman courts, as they had accused Paul in Corinth (Acts 18:12-17) and as they were to accuse Polycarp in Smyrna itself (*Martyrdom of Polycarp* 13:1); but his bitterness might have some quite other cause; and as to the false apostles of Ephesus (2:2) we are completely in the dark. It is unwise to attempt to interpret all the evidence of the seven letters within one simple framework. There seem from his description of them to have been some in the churches, those under the influence of "Jezebel" and Nicolaitan/"Balaamite" teaching, who directly opposed John on the issue of the imperial cult and its relevance to Christians. The lukewarmness and flagging zeal of which he complains in all the churches except Smyrna and Philadelphia may have led many to take the easier line of acquiescence in it (2:4, 3:1-2, 3:15-17). This malaise may have many causes, but it has to be tackled, and all the churches have to be strengthened, if they are to be able to face the crisis which John sees to be inevitable. His chief weapon in this is his vision, with its powerful images through which the readers may be enabled to interpret and so respond to their situation.

To conclude, then: we have seen that the images of Christ and the images of the adversaries are developed in strikingly similar ways. In the first, conventional images of the Messiah were given an added dimension in terms of God, and further related to the "facts of Jesus", the pattern of death and resurrection. Now, correspondingly, conventional images of human wickedness, wicked empires and wicked cities, have been given first their "heavenly" dimension in terms of the dragon and then a new direction over against the vision of Christ itself, so that the adversaries are seen cast in their darkness by the light of the Lamb. The imagery thus constructed is a powerful artistic creation and one with great polemical force and considerable social implications: the dualist structure of the imagery is a call to accept separation from the world, and John's voice is the voice of the ghetto.

Appendix: the Number of the Beast

No one who discusses the adversaries of the Apocalypse can avoid, or resist, tackling the puzzle of the number/name of the beast. In 13:17-18 the beast is said to have a "name" which is also a "number": the number is six hundred and sixty-six, and it calls for wisdom to reckon it out. Clearly, what we have here is a piece of number symbolism. Before the invention of arabic numerals, the same figures did duty as letters and as numbers in Hebrew, Greek, and Latin: what we call "Roman numerals" being the most familiar example. Thus a number written down could also "spell" something, and conversely a written word could be "added up". The usual approach to solving the riddle of the number of the beast is to see if that number "spells" the name of one of the Roman emperors (for the name of the beast is on its heads in 13:1, and in 17:9 these seven heads are kings, with the last of them the incarnation of the beast himself). This would also, of course, be an indication of the date of the Apocalypse, from the identity of the emperor whom John sees at the heart of the expected attack on the churches.

There are, however, three main obstacles in the way of this solution of the number-riddle. First, one must decide in which language the symbolism works: Latin, Greek, or Hebrew. Secondly, one must decide how the number is to be computed: whether cumulatively, to "add up" to six hundred and sixty-six; or consecutively, with six hundred-sixty-six in sequence; or, indeed, triangularly, for six hundred and sixty-six is a triangle of thirty-six, so that that could be the significant number. Thirdly, Roman emperors had a large number of names by which they might be known, not to mention titles: for example, "Caligula" was Gaius Julius Caesar Germanicus, Nero was Nero Claudius Caesar, and Domitian was Titus Flavius Domitianus.

Despite all this, solutions can be offered. We can extract "Nero" by taking the Greek *Neron Kaisar,* transliterating it into Hebrew and adding that up (it will not work in Greek); we can get "Domitian" by way of finding the abbreviations of his name and titles on his coinage and adding them up; while the variant reading of the number as six hundred and sixteen yields "Gaius Caesar", Caligula. It cannot, however, be said that there is an immediate, obvious, or overwhelmingly convincing solution along these lines. Indeed, a former student of King's College London, T.V. Smith, worked out four rules for solving the puzzle: first, decide at the outset to whom the number/name refers; secondly, if his name does not add up to six hundred and sixty-six, add a title; thirdly, if it does not work in Greek, try Latin or Hebrew; and finally, do not be too particular about the spelling!

This may seem somewhat defeatist, or dismissive, or both. I would not rule out the possibility that the cryptogram could be cracked in this way, by John's readers. After all, they knew who was their contemporary ruler, by what name or titles he was known in their province and society, and in what language. We do not know these things, and so the key may be permanently lost to us. I wonder, though, if this line of approach is the right one anyway: does the number symbol serve simply to identify the beast in one particular manifestation, or is it rather an interpretation of him, a further indication of his true character as the author sees it? The number can be seen to have an immediate symbolic force: conventionally, the complete number or the number of perfection is thought to be the number seven, and we have seen how prominently patterns or cycles of seven feature in the structure of the Apocalypse; the beast, by contrast, is six-six-six, always incomplete, doomed to failure, or, as 17:11 puts it, "to perdition". Again, there is some evidence that the letters of the name "Jesus" could be added up to give the number eight hundred and eighty-eight; and also that eight became symbolically the number of resurrection, the first day of the new week; so then the beast who parodies the Lamb might bear his sixes as a sign of his ineffective imitation of the one whose number is eight.

The first known commentator on the number of the beast is Irenaeus of Lyons (ca. A.D. 130-200); Irenaeus, as we have seen, dated the Apocalypse in the reign of Domitian. He addresses the question of the number in *Adv. Haer.* V.29-30,[11] and, working

---

[11] He also considers the textual variant on the number as six hundred and sixteen, arguing against its being the original reading on the modern sounding principles of manuscript support and internal consistency, and explaining how the variant could have arisen in the course of copying the text.

on a cumulative computation, canvasses a number of possible names for the beast, none of them imperial names, finally expressing his preference for either "Teitan" or "Lateinos". In the end, however, Irenaeus declines positively to identify the beast: it is, he says, unnecessary to do so since when he comes we cannot fail to recognize him (Irenaeus was not, of course, concerned to use the cryptogram to establish the date of the Apocalypse, since he regards it as predictive prophecy). He is much more interested in the symbolic meaning of the number, as he finds it, and this time working consecutively: six hundred is the age of Noah before the Flood (Genesis 7:6), and therefore indicates the generation of wickedness and the time of judgment; sixty and six are the dimensions of Nebuchadnezzar's statue (Daniel 3:1), an image of idolatry, to be resisted by God's people. Six hundred and sixty-six is therefore a number which evokes ideas of human wickedness and of idolatry, and, we might add, of martyrdom and the wrath of God.

Irenaeus is nearer in time and culture to the author of the Apocalypse then we are, and so may also be closer in sympathy. His instinct is to see the number as a symbol which interprets rather than merely identifies the beast (though it may do the latter as well), and so I may appeal to his authority in my agnostic attitude to the number as serving to identify an imperial enemy. I wish, too, to suggest following him in another respect. I cannot think of any modern commentator who has followed Irenaeus in looking for the interpretative meaning of the symbol by following the numbers consecutively; and so it is worth an attempt.

By the first century B.C. the Ionian system of letter-number equivalence had become general for the Greek-speaking or writing world: the cursive or minuscule letters of the alphabet representing the units one to nine, the "tens" ten to ninety, and the "hundreds" one hundred to nine hundred. As there were not quite enough letters in the current alphabet to do the job, some obsolete letters of the earlier Greek alphabet were resurrected.[12]

---

[12]For this account of the number system, see *The Oxford Classical Dictionary,* Oxford, 1949, entry "Numbers I" by T.L. Heath; and B.M. Metzger, *The Text of the New Testament,* Oxford, 1964, p. 190, n. 1.

Following this system, the number six hundred is represented by
the letter chi, *ch;* sixty, unpromisingly, by xi, *x;* and six by either
the obsolete digamma or by final sigma, *s. Chs* is an obvious
abbreviation for *Christos,* and indeed is one of the *nomina
sacra,* special words which were given standard abbreviations
for the sake of reverence in the earliest New Testament manu-
scripts, and no doubt in other contexts too.[13] The number-letter
x has less immediate reference, but we find that *xulon,* "wood"
or "tree" is the word used for the cross of Christ in 1 Pet. 2:24
(quoted in Polycarp, *Epistle* 8:1), in Acts 5:30, 10:39, and 13:29,
and in Gal. 3:13, where his death is seen as bearing the curse of
Deut. 21:23 on "everyone who hangs on a tree" (this association
between the crucifixion of Jesus and the Deuteronomic curse is
also found in Jn. 19:31, in the Jews' request to Pilate that the
criminals' bodies be taken down before nightfall). In the epistle
of Barnabas, which may be contemporary with the Apocalypse,
two further scriptural analogies between "wood" and the cross
are drawn: with the prophecy of 2 Esdras 5:5 (Barnabas 12:1)
and with Moses' staff with the brazen serpent (Barnabas 12:5-7,
Num. 21:8-9). Clearly, *xulon* was not only a familiar term for
the cross as the gallows-tree, but also a term that was suggestive
typologically.

So the number becomes a symbol of Christ and his cross. If
the method of computing it seems fanciful in the extreme, it is
interesting to find that there is a similar number symbol worked
out in the same way and to the same result in Barnabas 9:7-8.
Abraham, according to Gen. 14:14, had three hundred and
eighteen servants, and, as Barnabas reads the numbers consecutively, ten gives the letter iota, *i;* eight gives eta, *ē;* and three
hundred gives tau, *t. Iē* are the first letters of the name *Iesous,*
Jesus, and tau is the sign of the cross! Still, for Abraham the
patriarch to point forward to Christ and his cross, through a
judicious hiring of the right number of servants, is one thing; for
the beast to bear that symbol is quite another. Yet the name that

[13]For *nomina sacra,* see J.H. Greenlee, *Introduction to New Testament Textual
Criticism,* Grand Rapids, 1964, p. 30f.

the beast bears is said in 13:1 and 17:3 to be a blasphemous name, and we have seen that one dimension to John's portrait of him is that he is a parody of the Lamb, falsely claiming his status and his rôle. What is light with the Lamb is shadow in the beast; if he is a mirror-image, it is a distorting mirror, and it may seem appropriate that the number of his name is a further indication of his true character.[14]

[14]Time in the lectures and space here preclude a comparable discussion of the other cryptogram of the Apocalypse: the interpretation of the heads of the beast as seven kings in 17:9-11. In theory, this should be simply solved, and the date of the Apocalypse thereby established, from the imperial succession (granted that John is more concerned with the beast to come than with the king who now is in v. 10; this could be seen as his adopting the apocalyptic convention of "predicting" from a standpoint taken up in the past). Yet there are difficulties in this calculation: whether to include Julius Caesar, not technically a "king" but indubitably part of the succession; how many, if any, to include from the pretenders of the "year of four emperors", A.D. 68-69. One clear solution is to take the five emperors from Augustus to Nero and to date the Apocalypse in that year of turmoil, amid rumors, current in the East, of the return of Nero (Tacitus, *Histories* I.2, II.8-9; Suetonius, *Vita Caes.* Nero 57): a popular hope for many, but for Christians the gravest threat. The traditional Domitian dating could be established by taking the same five, omitting all the pretenders, identifying Vespasian as the supposed "present" emperor, with Titus (A.D. 79-81) as the one briefly to come, and then Domitian as the one to come, seen by the seer as Nero come again.Once again, no doubt John and his readers could make the calculation in their own terms: they knew (usually) who was ruling them; but also once again we should insist that the main force of the symbol is to interpret rather than simply to identify. The beast is many-headed, perhaps even specifically seven-headed, first and foremost because he is the dragon's beast; and he is "come again" with his mortal wound healed first and foremost because he parodies Christ. The last king who is the beast incarnate certainly had an identity as one of the emperors, but it is more important to the seer to reveal to the churches the threat to their faith which this king represents.

4

The Lamb's Army[1]

We have so far sought to show how, through his use of
imagery, the author of the Apocalypse interprets the conflict
which he expects to arise between the Christian churches and
the power of Rome. It is the climax of the whole history of
hostility of wicked cities and empires towards the people of
God; it is a manifestation of the cosmic conflict between the
dragon and the creator god; and at its heart is the conflict of
rival claims, for the Lamb and for the beast who is his parody
image. It is open to question whether the author speaks in this
way to or for his readers: whether they share his sense of
alienation and expectation of conflict, but need to be helped to
understand and so to face it; or whether they regard their
contemporary society as a matter of indifference and need to be
persuaded of its real nature. Either way, the author expects that
in the event they will come to be of his mind, for, as we
emphasized in the first chapter, his expectation is of martyrdom
on a massive scale: the harlot Babylon will be "drunk" with the
blood of the saints (17:6). We turn, then, to examine how the
author interprets this expected experience of the deaths of God's
people.

[1]This lecture was delivered on the day of the announcement of the award of the 1984
Nobel Peace Prize to Bishop Desmond Tutu of South Africa, graduate and Fellow of
King's College London, an event commemorated with appreciation at the lecture.

The experience of martyrdom, of suffering and dying precisely for being true to the faith (rather than suffering as a judgment for disloyalty to it) was not, of course, new with Christianity. The Jews had come to terms with it, in particular in the Maccabean period with the attack on their faith through the policies of the Hellenizing king Antiochus IV Epiphanes of Syria from 168 B.C. The book of Daniel in the Old Testament is a reflection on that experience, and subsequent reflection often emerges through a retelling of the Maccabean story.

Five distinct lines of approach may be found in Jewish literature of the period of the beginnings of Christianity. First, death may be regarded as the ultimate display of fidelity to God and to his law: "thou shalt love the Lord thy God ... with all thy soul", your life, "even if he take thy soul (away)" (Deut. 6:4, the *Sh'ma',* as interpreted by Rabbi Akiba and fulfilled in his martyrdom,[2] and earlier exemplified by those who were slaughtered rather than profane the Sabbath in 1 Macc. 2:29-38). Secondly, the death of the righteous is seen to call for God's retribution upon the persecutors, which may be confidently expected (as by the seven brothers in 2 Macc. 7:15-17, 34-37). Conversely, the martyr may also confidently expect that God will vindicate him by giving him life: the idea of life after death as other than merely a shadowy existence arose late in the history of Israel's faith, and the hope of resurrection was born in the experience of persecution, as in Dan. 12:2, "many of those who sleep in the dust of the earth shall awake", and 2 Macc. 7:9, 14. Fourthly, the suffering of God's people may be seen as an inevitable part of the convulsions of the present world-order before its end and God's establishing of his new kingdom (thus in apocalyptic literature such as 1 Enoch 47:1-4, and in Mark 13, where there will be "tribulation" involving God's elect, vv. 19f., but "he who endures to the end will be saved", v. 13.) Finally, in some areas there also developed a conviction that the suffering of the righteous had a vicarious effect: they suffered on behalf of their people, either as a propitiation, to bear the wrath

[2]Babylon Talmud *Berakoth* 61*b.*

of God upon that people's sin and so to exhaust it (2 Macc. 7:38), or as an atoning sacrifice for their sins (4 Macc. 6:29, another retelling of the story of Eleazar and the seven brothers, in which Eleazar prays "Be merciful unto thy people, and let our punishment be a satisfaction on their behalf. Make my blood their purification, and take my soul to ransom their souls"; cf. also 4 Macc. 1:11, 17:21f.)

These ideas were not logically related or worked out to provide a "theory" of martyrdom, as, for instance, by relating the fourth and fifth to argue that the suffering of the righteous in the final tribulation is necessary to avert the wrath from the rest of God's people; by and large they remain as distinct ideas, different ways of approaching a variously recurring experience. Most of them are reflected in the Apocalypse of John, in its approach to the expectation of a new persecution. Those who die are, first, those who "loved not their lives even unto death" (12:11), and Antipas who has already died in Pergamum is the "faithful one" (2:13). Secondly, the martyrs seen under the altar of heaven cry out for the avenging of their blood (6:10), and in the cycle of the final judgment, the cycle of the bowls of wrath, that retribution is given (thus in the declaration of the angel of water and the confirmation from the altar of heaven whence the cry for vengeance had earlier come, 16:5-7; retribution for the blood of God's servants is also celebrated by a great multitude in heaven in 19:1-3). Thirdly, confidence of vindication in the giving of life to those who die is clearly expressed: in that vision of the souls of the martyrs as already under the altar of heaven in 6:9, in the restoration and exaltation of the two witnesses of 11:11-12, and in the "first resurrection" of 20:4. Again, martyrdom is seen in the context of the total eschatological suffering in the reminder to the martyrs in heaven that the number of their fellow-servants and brethren to be killed must be completed (6:11), in the description of the great multitude of 7:14 as those who have emerged from the "great tribulation", and in the warning to the church of Smyrna that it will "have tribulation" and must be "faithful unto death" (2:10). Only the fifth approach is lacking. The martyrs themselves are described as "spotless" (14:5) and are seen in their robes washed white

(7:14, cf. 6:11), but their deaths are not described as sacrifices availing for others, nor as achieving others' purification. This is congruous with what we noted earlier, the absence of sacrificial interpretation of the death of the Lamb, and it may also relate to a question to which we shall return, whether the martyrs are for John a distinct group within God's people or whether they effectively comprise God's people (is there, in short, a "people of God" apart from the martyrs for whom their deaths might have any vicarious effect?).

Thus far the author may be seen to interpret the experience of martyrdom in terms which may be described as conventional. There are, however, two lines of approach which are distinctively his own. First, he repeatedly describes those who die as "witnesses". Antipas, who has already died, is "my witness, my faithful one" (2:13); the two figures who are put to death and vindicated in 11:3-12 are "my two witnesses" (11:3); the harlot is drunk with the blood of saints and "the blood of the witnesses of Jesus" (17:6); and witness is made by those who "loved not their lives even unto death" (12:11). It is, of course, the Greek word *martus,* witness, that gives us our English word "martyr," with a shift of meaning from one who gives evidence, as in a court of law, to one who dies for the faith, that death being his witness to it. It is often suggested that this shift of language occurs in the Apocalypse, and indeed that the seer is responsible for it. Some English translations implicitly take this view and anticipate the shift in meaning: the RSV reads "the blood of the martyrs of Jesus" at 17:6. The view is explicitly taken by a predecessor in the Tuohy Chair, W.H.C. Frend, who concludes that in the Apocalypse *martus* appears "in the technical sense of being a blood witness, the sense it was to retain from now on".[3] However, the ideas of witness and of death are probably still distinct in the book: those under the altar have been slaughtered "for" their witness (6:9), as have those who have been beheaded in 20:4; and indeed the author himself bears witness in 1:2 and is given witness to bear in 22:16, and, although he is a "sharer in the

[3] *Martyrdom and Persecution in the Early Church,* Oxford, 1965, p. 91.

tribulation" in 1:9 and in exile on Patmos, he is not dead! The martyrs' witness is not, then, simply identified with their deaths, but it is pre-eminently those who die who are called "witnesses".[4] John's other characteristic description of the martyrs is as victors or conquerors. Each of the seven letters to the churches concludes with a promise held out to *ho nikōn,* "the conqueror" (thus 2:7, 2:11, 2:17, 2:26-28, 3:5, 3:12, 3:21), and some of these promises are expressly fulfilled in the later vision of the martyrs. In the letter to the church of Smyrna the promise to the conqueror is that he "shall not be hurt by the second death" (2:11); and so in 20:4-6 it is the martyrs raised in the first resurrection over whom "the second death has no power". For Laodicea the risen Christ promises the conqueror that he will "sit with me on my throne" (3:21), and in 20:4, 6 it is the risen martyrs who reign with Christ. For Sardis the promise is that the conqueror will be "clad ... in white garments" (3:5), as we see the martyrs in heaven given white robes in 6:11 and those who have come out of the great tribulation "clothed in white robes" in 7:9. The correlation is not possible for all the promises, but from what we have it is reasonable to conclude that "the conqueror" is most obviously, if not exclusively, a designation for the martyr.

This is consistent, too, with the way that the martyrs are presented in John's vision as victorious warriors. In 12:11 the victory in the war in heaven is achieved by the blood of the Lamb and by those who "loved not their lives even unto death". In 14:1-5 the Lamb is seen with his hundred and forty-four thousand followers, described as those "who have not defiled themselves with women, for they are chaste" (14:4). This description is unlikely to be a charter for Christian asceticism: it is more likely that the Lamb's followers are presented as prepared for holy war, for which chastity was (at least in ideal theory) an element in total commitment. Uriah the Hittite would not lie

---

[4]For a detailed discussion of this question of language, see A.A. Trites, "*Martus* and Martyrdom in the Apocalypse", *Novum Testamentum* XV, 1973, pp. 72-80, and *The New Testament Concept of Witness,* Cambridge, 1977, pp. 154-74.

with his wife Bathsheba, thus foiling David's plan to conceal his adultery with her, while "the ark and Israel and Judah are in booths" prepared for battle (2 Sam. 11:11). These hundred and forty-four thousand warriors are presumably the same group as that number "sealed" in 7:4-8, whose identity is much debated, for chapter seven appears to introduce two groups: first of twelve thousand from each of the twelve tribes of Israel, then "a great multitude which no man could number from every nation" who are those "who have come out of the great tribulation" (7:9-17). Jewish and gentile Christians? Chapter seven has, however, that pattern of transition from what John "hears" to what he "sees" which we observed in 5:5-6 to mark a transition from the terms of traditional expectation to its new Christian content: the expected Lion was shown to be the Lamb. Here what is announced is the familiar hope for the establishing of the people of God in the new age; what is seen is those who have borne the eschatological suffering. There are not two groups: the new, or true, Israel of God is found in the multitude of martyrs, who are the Lamb's "noble army".[5]

The martyrs are to die for their faith; the Lamb has already been slain. It would be extraordinary if the seer left these two facts unrelated, and of course he does not. Those under the altar of heaven in 6:9 have been "slaughtered", as has the Lamb in 5:6 (and the head of the beast in 13:3): the same word is used and the analogy clearly drawn. (Indeed, it may be because "slaughter" was the obviously appropriate term for the violent deaths of the martyrs that John chose to use it for the death of the Lamb.) Again, the two witnesses are put to death in "the great city which is allegorically called Sodom and Egypt, where their Lord was crucified" (11:8). But the analogy drawn by the author between the deaths of Christ and of Christians is not simply an analogy of fact but of interpretation, for the language which we have seen used to interpret their deaths is also used of him. As

---

[5] Possibly, though not so clearly, the martyrs also constitute the white-clothed armies of heaven who accompany Christ as the rider on the white horse in 19:14.

Antipas of Pergamum is "my witness, my faithful one" (2:13), so Jesus Christ is "the faithful witness, the first-born of the dead" (1:5), and the witness that they bear is his: "the witness of Jesus" (12:17, 20:4),[6] though again it is not exclusively they who bear it, for prophecy, including John's own message, is also "the testimony of Jesus" (1:2,9; 19:10). So, too, as the martyr is most obviously "the conqueror" of the seven letters, the Lamb also "has conquered" so that he can open the sealed book (5:5), and he is worthy to do so because he was slaughtered (5:9).

As we have seen in the interaction of the image of Christ and the images of the adversaries, reflection on the facts of Jesus has served again to extend and develop inherited ideas. The deaths of Christian martyrs may indeed be the outcome of their faithfulness, may call alike for retribution and vindication, and may be an inevitable part of the great tribulation, but because they are now associated with the death of Jesus that cannot be all that there is to say about them. What the martyrs are to experience is what Jesus has experienced, and so their experience is given a new language and content in the light of his: it is not passive resistance but effective action. That death should be described as "victory" is a paradox, because it seems more obviously an ultimate defeat, but the language functions in the context of the author's perception of his situation in adversarial, dualistic terms: the city *versus* the people of God, dragon *versus* God, Lamb *versus* beast. What is needed is not a moral resolution in terms of atonement for sin, but a solution in terms of power and conquest; and because for John the central effective action is the death of the Lamb, death becomes victory for him and for his followers. "Witness" is a more ambiguous description, for it could be construed as witness to persuade and/or to convict: the Lamb and his followers could be thought of as testifying to men to convince them of the truth, or testifying against men, to God, to convict them. In the polarized situation

---

[6]This point of connection remains substantially the same whether the genitive of the phrase is construed as subjective or objective: the witness borne *by* Jesus, which the martyrs reaffirm (cf. 1 Tim. 6:13), or witness borne by them *to* him.

as the author perceives it, it is probable that the latter is the correct construction. For John, the witness of the Lamb and the martyrs succeeds not when men respond to it (it must be doubtful if he thought the adversaries capable of response) but when God upholds it. Christ as "the faithful witness" is not so only in his death but in that he is "the firstborn of the dead", raised, vindicated and exalted by God. The archetypal two witnesses are not persuasive in their testimony in the great city (11:7, 10), but having been slain there, they are raised and exalted to strike its inhabitants with an awe that is unavailing terror (11:11-13)[7]

As the martyrs in their deaths share the victory of Christ, it is appropriate that they should also share in the consequences of his victory: his reign; and so they do. In the letter to the church at Thyatira, the conqueror is promised that he will rule the nations "with a rod of iron" (2:27), as will the rider on the white horse (19:15). Most dramatically, though, the martyrs are shown to share the reign of Christ in the millennial kingdom: "I saw the souls of those who had been beheaded[8] for their testimony to Jesus and for the word of God, and who had not worshipped the beast or its image . . . they came to life and reigned with Christ a thousand years" (20:4). The inclusion of the millennial reign in the seer's vision of the future is, of course, a striking feature of the Apocalypse, and provokes something of an

---

[7]Substantially the same conclusion is reached by J.P.M. Sweet, "Maintaining the testimony of Jesus", in W. Horbury and B. McNeil, eds., *Suffering and Martyrdom in the New Testament,* Cambridge, 1981, pp. 101-117, though he sees some hint of the persuasive power of the martyrs' witness in the later reference to "the healing of the nations" (22:2). In general, however, witness "is ultimately victorious not by the moral effect of the suffering it incurs, but by God's vindication, which shatters the opposition" (p. 101).

[8]The verb *pelekizō,* found only here in the New Testament and Septuagint, literally means "cut off with an axe", and the noun *pelekus* is used of the axes in the Roman *fasces:* the bundle of rods with an axe carried by lictors before the higher magistrates as a symbol of their legal authority. John's choice of this verb, unusual in its context but highly evocative, may be to indicate again that the martyrs' deaths will be incurred in conflict with the Roman state.

exegetical division. For some readers, it is the most important feature of the book, of immediate and personal concern;[9] for others it is an embarrassment, or at best a puzzle. It seems to interrupt the natural sequence of the last few chapters. After our stage (7), the cycle of the bowls of wrath and the woes of the end, the great adversaries are defeated: the great city falls (chapter 18), the beast and the false prophet are the rider's prisoners of war (19:19-21), even the devil is bound (20:1-3a). In chapters 21-22:5 the new creation is established, with its imagery of the holy city, of Eden and of paradise. Between the two, though, in an action-packed nine verses, there intervenes the millennial kingdom and its sequel in the release of Satan, the invasion of Gog and Magog, the resurrection of all the dead and judgment. We may justifiably pause to consider the reason for this apparent interruption, and the function of the idea of the millennium as distinct from the New Age.

Millenarian belief is often regarded as characteristic of fringe sects or of protest movements;[10] and it is essentially a sectarian idea, defining boundaries in terms of time, place and those involved in the event. There are clear distinctions between those who belong in the millennium and those who are excluded from it. As an "exclusive" idea, it can be seen to be natural to those who feel themselves "excluded" from their wider society, whether that society is defined in religious, political or cultural terms. Marginal people, feeling themselves excluded, accept that dividing boundaries exist, but reverse them to find their own positive identity as the "included ones" in the millennium. However, if millenarian belief has come to seem characteristic of the sect rather than the Church, this would not be true of the early period of Christian history, where the roll-call of millenarians is a noble one, including the author of the Epistle of

---

[9]For example, A.A. Hoekema, *The Bible and the Future,* Exeter, 1979, despite the breadth of its title, is dominated by the exposition of millenarian views, which have their own technical vocabulary.

[10]It is chronicled in this respect, especially in the mediaeval and reformation periods, by N. Cohn, *The Pursuit of the Millennium,* London, 1957.

Barnabas (chapter 15), Justin Martyr (*Dialogue* 80-81), Irenaeus (*Adv. Haer.* V.32-36), Papias (in Eusebius *H.E.* III.39.11-13) and Tertullian (*Adv. Marc.* III.24, IV.31). As held by Tertullian's Montanist fellow believers the belief had a sectarian context, but it would seem that in this early period it was very widely held in the Church as part of the Christian hope for the future; understandably perhaps in a time when all Christians were to some extent marginal people in their wider society, open to suspicion and the threat of persecution. One formidable exception, however, was Origen, who experienced persecution at first hand yet rejected this idea of a limited reign of Christ on earth as incompatible with his vision of *apokatastasis,* the total restoration of the cosmos (*De Princ..* I.6.3). His disciple Eusebius echoed Origen's disdain for millenarianism and with it, as we have seen, for the Apocalypse of John, but he instead found it incompatible with his acclamation of Constantine as effecting the rule of Christ on earth (*Oration on the Tricennalia* 2.1-5); with the Church poised to influence the government of the Empire, hope of a new reign on earth hardly seemed relevant![11]

Millenarian belief has come, then, in many quarters of the Church to seem something of an embarrassment. One way of relieving this (for which indeed Origen provides a precedent) is to regard it as part of Christianity's cultural and spiritual legacy from Judaism, an element of the Church's past but not of its distinctive faith, and so dispensable. In the construction of his Apocalypse John could be seen to be conditioned by a structure given him in scripture, for his last chapters seem to follow the later chapters of the book of Ezekiel: in chapter 18 his vision of the fall of the great city echoes Ezekiel 27-28 on the fall of Tyre, and the binding of the dragon in 20:1-3 echoes Ezekiel 29-32

[11]For a survey of patristic views, see H. Bietenhard, "The Millennial Hope in the Early Church," *Scottish Journal of Theology* 6, 1953, pp. 12-30; for the broader question of whether Early Christianity should be characterized as a millenarian movement, see J.G. Gager, *Kingdom and Community,* Englewood Cliffs, N. J., 1975, and R. Scroggs, "The Earliest Christian Communities as Sectarian Movement," in J. Neusner, ed., *Christianity, Judaism, and other Greco-Roman Cults,* vol. II, Leiden, 1975, and "The Sociological Interpretation of the New Testament: the Present State of Research," *N.T.S.* 26, 1980, pp. 164-179.

with the consigning of the dragon Egypt to the pit; Gog and Magog in 20:8 obviously come from Ezekiel 38-39, while the vision of the new Jerusalem in chapter 21-22:5 derives in part from the vision of the future in Ezekiel 40-48. In the sequence of Ezekiel, between chapters 32 and 38, there would intervene, *inter alia,* the vision of the valley of dry bones restored to life (Ezekiel 37), and the Apocalypse's "first resurrection" (20:4-6) might seem to come into the pattern in a deliberate correspondence. Or else, it might be argued more generally, without appealing to a precise literary connection, that although the idea of a messianic kingdom as distinct from the new age has no precedent in the Old Testament, and, in relation to the gospels, we may talk interchangeably of "the kingdom of God" or "the messianic age", there are some indications of such a distinction in Jewish and Christian literature from the end of the first century; maybe in an attempt to harmonize the traditional Davidic hope of an earthly kingdom with the transcendent eschatology of the new earth or the new aeon.[12]

It may be noted, however, that the conception of a distinction between the messianic age and the new aeon did not involve a consensus on the duration of the former. 2 Esdras 7:28 speaks of four hundred years; Strack-Billerbeck gives a long list of differing opinions among rabbis from the end of the first to the fourth century: forty years, seventy years, one hundred, four hundred, one thousand, two thousand, seven thousand, two thousand four hundred and sixty—all calculations derived somehow from

[12]Examples usually given are 1 Enoch 93:1-10 and 91:12-17, Sibylline Oracles III: 652-731, 2 Baruch 29-30 and 40, 2 Esdras 7:28-43; all of which pose the usual problems of distinguishing original Jewish ideas and Christian influence or interpolation, and indeed possible influence from the Apocalypse of John itself. For discussion, see J. Bailey, "The Temporary Messianic Reign in the Literature of Early Judaism," *J.B.L.* 53, 1934, pp. 170-187; J. Daniélou, *The Theology of Jewish Christianity,* London, 1964, pp. 377-404; and articles by E. Lohse, *chilias, chilioi* in *The Theological Dictionary of the New Testament,* vol. ix, Grand Rapids, Mich., 1974, pp. 466-471; and C. Brown, *"NUMBER, chilias, chilioi,"* in *A Dictionary of New Testament Theology,* vol. 2, Exeter, 1976, pp. 697-704.

a scriptural text.[13] The calculation of a thousand year reign relates to the idea of a "cosmic week": the six days of God's work in Gen. 1:1–2:3 are interpreted as the six thousand year duration of creation, followed by the "sabbath" thousand and then the eighth or timeless day.[14]

It can therefore be argued that the seer of the Apocalypse is articulating in one way a widely and variously held belief; he is not the originator or source of it, and in fact the idea is to some extent in tension with other and more characteristic elements of his thought. For instance, his vision of the millennial kingdom would seem to be a vision of the coming reign of Christ, when the devil will have been bound and the dead raised to be with him. Yet the Christ of Revelation is not a figure of the future: the son of man is now among the candlesticks which are the seven churches (1:12f.), in the letters encouraging, warning, judging them and knocking at the door (3:20); and the Lamb stands now in heaven, having conquered (5:5f.). Congruously the martyrs who are seen in analogy with him do not have to wait for future resurrection to be with him: the souls of the slain already wait under the heavenly altar (6:9); the great multitude of those who have come through the great tribulation are already seen before the throne and the Lamb (7:9) during the opening of the seven seals, the preliminary and partial woes; the two witnesses are taken straight to heaven (11:11f.), again during the preliminary cycle of the trumpets; and it is announced that "Blessed are the dead who die in the Lord henceforth" (14:13). So too, although in 20:2f. the devil is to be bound for the thousand years, he has actually already been defeated in 12:9,

[13]H. L. Strack and P. Billerbeck, *Kommentar zum Neuen Testament als Talmud und Midrasch,* Munich, 1926, vol. III, pp. 823-827.

[14]The calculation is clearly made in Barnabas 15:4 where Genesis 1-2 is linked with Psalm 90:4: God works for six days and the seventh is the Lord's day; but according to the psalm "a thousand years in thy sight are but as yesterday." The "day" of God's rest is the time of the rule of his Son, and then God will make an "eighth day which is the beginning of another world." Daniélou derives the calculation of the thousand years differently: from the intended span of Adam's life in Paradise according to Jubilees 4:29-30 (*op. cit.,* pp. 390f.).

and the cry went up immediately then that "Now ... the kingdom of our God and the authority of his Christ have come" (12:10).

These are precisely the points taken up by Augustine in his influential interpretation of the Apocalypse in *De Civitate Dei* XX.7-9 (an interpretation taken over, broadmindedly, from the *Commentary* of the Donatist Tyconius). The millennium, Augustine argues, is not a vision of the future but an insight into the present. Christ's reign begins with his first coming, not his second, and his kingdom is the Church, where those live who have come to life from sin through baptism and from which the souls of the dead saints are not separated; the devil is bound in the sense of Mark 3:27, that the strong man's goods are already being plundered. In this way the vision of the Apocalypse would be brought into harmony with the only other New Testament reference to the reign specifically of Christ as distinct from that of God: 1 Cor. 15:24-28, where Paul affirms that Christ reigns now, as the first fruits of the dead, subjecting all things to himself until the end when he delivers the kingdom to God. Augustine's view is still canvassed, as by Colin Brown, who extends it further: the binding of the devil "that he should deceive the nations no more" (20:3) is achieved in the preaching of the gospel to all nations.[15] Yet, influential and attractive as this line of interpretation is, we must dissent from it. In chapter 20 we must surely find a vision of the future, following as it does our stage (7), the cycle of the bowls of wrath which is the unbroken cycle of final judgment with its closing declaration that "it is done!" (16:17) and the fall of the great city (16:17-19). The seer now seems to be looking beyond the present situation, and it must surely be accepted that his vision of the future included the maybe by then widespread idea of a messianic reign. That does not, of course, mean that the thousand year duration should be taken literally, for other numbers in the Apocalypse are obviously symbolic (silence in heaven "for about half an hour", 8:1; the exposure of the witnesses' corpses for "three and a half days",

---

[15] *Dictionary of New Testament Theology,* op. cit., p. 702.

11:11; the woman protected for "one thousand two hundred and sixty days", 12:6).[16] The force of the identificaton of this special time as "a thousand years" is to interpret it as the sabbath time, the day of the Lord; and in the context of the Christian vision the Lord is "the Lord Jesus" whose messianic reign is shortly to begin (21:20).

Two final observations may be made. John gives content to his vision of the millennial kingdom in the light of his own interests. The time of the kingdom is the time of the martyrs (20:4); a notion apparently without parallel. The inclusion of the millennium in his scheme is not a mechanical (and so dispensable?) taking over of a conventional eschatological sequence: its inclusion has a special function in relation to his especial estimation of the martyrs. Their special rôle requires a special reward, and those who are supremely the "excluded ones" of the present world have their exclusive place in the future. Secondly, the tensions which we have noted above exist. The millennial kingdom is part of John's hope for the future, but in his view of the present, elements of the future hope are already realized. This tension is not carelessness or muddle or incompetence; it is an inevitable tension because the Messiah to whose reign John looks forward is a Messiah who has already come: Christ the rider on the white horse, the avenger of wrath in the final judgment, is also Christ the Lamb who has been slain and Christ the one like a son of man, present among the churches.[17] If the idea of the millennium is part of John's cultural inheritance he has not simply passed it on in turn, but has made his own, and his own Christian, sense of it.

To return to the mainstream of our discussion: the author of the Apocalypse interprets the martyrdom which he expects in terms of his understanding of Christ; the martyrs are seen "in the light of the Lamb", the lamp of the heavenly city in which God

---

[16]2 Pet. 3:8 shows that Psalm 90:4 might be appealed to to show the irrelevance rather than the precision of calculation!

[17]Contrast the judgment of Rudolf Bultmann that in Revelation "the peculiar 'between-ness' of Christian existence has not been grasped" (*Theology of the New Testament,* vol 2, London, 1955, p. 175).

"will wipe away every tear from their eyes, and death shall be no more" (21:4). As he is witness and conqueror, and will reign, so will they bear witness, conquer and reign. We have here one major development of the theme of the martyr as the follower and imitator of Christ which is variously expressed in other parts of the New Testament and early Christian literature. The author of Luke-Acts gives his account of the death of Stephen the first martyr so as to make the parallels with the account of the death of Jesus in his gospel unmistakable: Stephen prays "Lord, do not hold this sin against them" (Acts 7:60) as Jesus had prayed "Father, forgive them; for they know not what they do" (Lk. 23:34); commits himself, "Lord Jesus, receive my spirit" (7:59) as Jesus' final words were "Father, into thy hands I commit my spirit" (23:46); and as Jesus could confidently assure the penitent thief that "today you will be with me in Paradise" (23:43) so Stephen could "see the heavens opened, and the Son of man standing at the right hand of God" (7:56).[18] The same deliberate patterning of the account of a martyr's death upon the passion narrative is found in the report of the death of Polycarp of Smyrna in A.D. 155/6: "an example of the martyrdom which resembles the Gospel story" (*Martyrdom of Polycarp* 1.1).[19] With Ignatius of Antioch (d. ca. A.D. 115) the martyr takes the rôle upon himself, in forbidding the Roman Christians to make any attempt to prevent his death, but rather "Permit me to be an imitator of the passion of my God" (Ignatius, *To the Romans* 6.3).

With Ignatius, however, we have an indication of a darker side to this interpretation of the martyr as the imitator of Christ and of its consequences in the life of the early Church: the implication that because it is such an imitation martyrdom is to

[18]The difference, that Jesus' prayers are addressed to God the Father while Stephen's are addressed to the risen Lord Jesus, is, at least potentially, of great christological significance, since, in being addressed in prayer, Jesus is implicitly seen in the rôle of God.

[19]Details which point to the parallel include Polycarp's betrayal by a member of his household (*Martyrdom of Polycarp* 6.1-2), his arrest "at about supper time" (7.1), interrogation by an official called Herod (6.1, 8.2), and death on "a high Sabbath" (8.1, cf. John 19:31).

be sought or courted, and that the martyr is the supreme, even perhaps the exclusive, follower of the Lord.[20] So it is relevant to ask one final question: whether for the author of the Apocalypse it is only the martyr as the imitator and follower of the Lamb who is the true Christian, and whether he either expects all followers of Christ to perish in the coming conflict or disregards those who do not. It is fair to note again that the rôle of witness is not confined to the martyr, though it is pre-eminently his; that the promises to "the conqueror" of the letters are not all seen to be performed for the martyr of the vision, though several of them explicitly are; and that the end of John's vision is not the millennial kingdom where only the martyrs are raised to reign, but the New Jerusalem beyond it, where indeed is found the "tree of life" promised to the conqueror in the letter to Ephesus (22:2, cf. 2:7). Yet his expectation is of an extreme situation, and his main concern is with those who will suffer its extremity; they dominate his vision, at times it seems to the exclusion of all else. We cannot look to the author of the Apocalypse for an exposition of Christian living as the imitation of Christ by those who live everyday lives and may expect to die peacefully in their beds.[21]

---

[20]For discussion of the temptations of martyrdom and its varying assessment in the early Church, see H. Chadwick, *The Early Church,* Harmondsworth, 1967, pp. 28-31, and W. H. C. Frend, *Martyrdom and Persecution,* pp. 197-200, 288f., and 353-358.

[21]It is interesting briefly to note comparisons and contrasts between Revelation and the first epistle of Peter, since both documents anticipate persecution and in that context explore the theme of the imitation of Christ. For Peter as for John the expectation of suffering goes along with the expectation of the end: "the end of all things is at hand" (4:7, cf. 1:5), and that suffering is indeed a necessary preliminary to the end, since "the time has come for judgment to begin with the household of God" (4:17) and "the same experience of suffering is required of your brotherhood throughout the world" (5:9). In the epistle, too, a new dimension is given to the picture by the affirmation that the planned and effective act of salvation has taken place in the suffering and exaltation of Christ (1:18-21, cf. 1:10-11 where this is the realization of prophecy), and therefore Christian suffering can be accepted as the following of Christ's "example" (2:21, cf. 3:17-18, 4:1). Here again the hostile situation is the context for bearing witness, with the ambiguity of whether the function of witness is to persuade or to convict (3:15-16); but in 1 Peter the former seems more probable since he is optimistic about the capacity of the outside society to distinguish between good and evil and, at least to some extent, to act accordingly (2:12-15, cf. 3:13-14, where suffering precisely for doing right must remain a possibility). In the situation of a mixed marriage, too, the Christian wife may expect to

persuade her unbelieving husband "so that some, though they do not obey the word, may be won without a word by the behaviour of their wives" (3:1-2). Another striking difference between the two documents is that for Peter the imitation of Christ in suffering may be in the daily drudgery of the Christian servant to an unjust master and not just in the "drama" of persecution (2:18-21); and indeed there may be imitation in situations not involving suffering at all, as when the elders who are shepherds of "the flock of God" follow "the chief Shepherd" (5:1-4). The rôles of witness and imitator may be enacted in everyday life. Maybe the author of the epistle faced a less extreme situation than that of the seer of the Apocalypse; or maybe in his extremity he remained able to take a broader view.

5

The Songs of the Lamb

Our discussion of the Apocalypse has been developing in a recognizable order: from the author's images of Christ the Lamb to their reflection in the images of his adversaries and to their impact in the presentation of his army the martyrs. The latter are seen in his light, the former are cast by that light into their shadows, and thus the author interprets their respective rôles in the conflict in which he expects them to be engaged. The subject of this chapter may seem something of a digression, even an indulgence, but its inclusion may be justified on three grounds: first, that the language of worship is such a striking characteristic of the Apocalypse, with a legacy in subsequent Christian worship and in musical creation, that it deserves discussion in its own right; secondly, that worship is an issue in the conflict of claims which the author perceives in his situation, for, as we have seen, it is characteristic of the beast that he requires and is given worship (e.g., 13:4, 11), and to refuse that worship is to incur death (13:15), so that the martyrs of the millennial kingdom are defined as those "who had not worshipped the beast or its image and had not received its mark" (20:4). The third justification is that the subject is not in fact a digression at all, for the language of worship provides further illustration of the main theme of our discussion, and that in three respects.

The language of worship is, as we have observed, a striking

characteristic of the Apocalypse of John. At least eleven times his vision is punctuated by songs of praise or rejoicing,[1] and indeed the vision is enclosed in the context of worship. The seer describes himself as having been "in the Spirit on the Lord's day" (1:10). This could be the Sabbath of Yahweh the Lord God of Israel, but it is more probably the earliest reference to the Christian identification of "Sunday," the day of the Lord's resurrection. Paul asks for contributions from his gentile churches for the poor Christians of Jerusalem to be put aside "on the first day of every week" (1 Cor. 16:1-2); he does not, however, associate this practice with the meetings of the Corinthian church for their eucharistic meal (1 Cor. 11:17-34; compare Acts 20:7) or for mutual edification by prophecy and other speech or song (1 Cor. 14:26; it is not clear whether Paul is thinking of different occasions of meeting or whether a meeting of the Corinthian church might comprise all these forms of activity!), though such meetings would be an obvious occasion for the collection of charity. It is Justin Martyr (d.c a. A. D. 165) who provides us with the first description and explanation of the Christian Sunday, "the day of the Sun" and the first day of the week (*Apology* I.67), but the allusion in the Apocalypse may indicate that its commemoration had begun at least half a century before.[2] The description of the day as "the Lord's" or "the lordly day" (*hē kuriakē hēmera*) is itself interesting: the adjective is also used in the New Testament of the eucharist as "the Lord's supper" (1 Cor. 11:20), but outside the New Testament papyri and inscriptions show that it had a legal con-

---

[1]Identification, and so calculation, of the songs of the Apocalypse varies; we shall be drawing on the following passages: 4:8, 4:9-11, 5:8-10, 5:11-12, 5:13, 7:10, 7:11-12, 11:15-18, 14:2-3, 15:2-4, 19:1-4 and 19:6-8.

[2]Barnabas may provide near contemporary corroboration that "we keep the eighth day [*sic.* the first day of the new week] for rejoicing, in which also Jesus rose from the dead" (15:9), and Ignatius refers to his and his readers' predecessors as "no longer observing sabbaths but fashioning their lives after the Lord's day, on which our life also arose through him" (*To the Magnesians* 9:1). For a study of the early Christian observance of Sunday, see W. Rordorf, *Sunday,* London, 1968.

notation, identifying matters imperial: the imperial treasury or imperial finance, for example.[3] Paul's use of the adjective may indicate that it served simply as a concise and convenient means for Christians to associate their practices with their Lord, but in a context like that of the Apocalypse where "matters imperial" were, to say the least, a sensitive issue, its use could have a polemical edge: the Christian day is truly "imperial", truly "lordly", because it commemorates the true Lord.[4]

John closes the account of his vision with a prayer: "Come, Lord Jesus!" (22:20). This is equivalent to Paul's prayer *Maranatha,* "Our Lord, come!", which, similarly followed by a grace, closes 1 Corinthians (16:22). Preserved by Paul in its original Aramaic, transliterated rather than translated into Greek, this is one of the earliest prayers of the Church. It is found in *Didache* 10:6 as part of the liturgy of the Eucharist. The seer who was "in the Spirit on the Lord's day" concludes, then, with the eucharistic prayer that came to belong to that day. Eucharistic allusion has also been found in the Apocalypse in the promise to the church of Laodicea that "if anyone hears my voice ... I will come in to him and eat with him, and he with me" (3:20). Some scholars have taken up these and other supposed allusions to argue that the structure of certain chapters of the book, or all of it, is based upon liturgical patterns. We shall not discuss such theories here, believing that the structure and form of the Apocalypse can be adequately explained without them; but that they are put forward is congruous with the importance of worship in its content.[5]

[3] Evidence in A. Deissman, *Light from the Ancient East,* reprinted Grand Rapids, Mich., 1965, pp. 357-361.

[4] Deissman pursues this line in connection, further, with evidence for the marking of a day, perhaps once a month, as *Sebastē*, "Augustus Day", raising the possibility that the distinctive title "Lord's Day" may have been connected with conscious feelings of protest against the cult of the Emperor. *Ibid.,* p. 359.

[5] Studies of liturgical influence on the Apocalypse include M.H. Shepherd, *The Pascal Liturgy and the Apocalypse,* London, 1960, and P. Prigent, *Apocalypse et Liturgie,* Neuchatel, 1964; a useful survey of recent study of the hymns in the book is provided by D.R. Carnegie, "Worthy is the Lamb: the Hymns in Revelation" in *Christ the Lord: Studies in Christology presented to Donald Guthrie,* ed. H.H. Rowden, Leicester, 1982.

To whom, then, is all this worship addressed? In the opening vision of heaven it is naturally addressed to God, as "he who sits on the throne" (4:3). The four living creatures around the throne ceaselessly praise him, "Holy, holy, holy, is the Lord God Almighty, who was and is and is to come!" (4:8); and the twenty-four elders respond in acclamation, "Worthy art thou, our Lord and God, to receive glory and honour and power" as creator (4:11). In the following chapter, however, on the introduction of the Lamb, worship is addressed to him, in very similar terms. The four creatures and the twenty-four elders sing a "new song" acclaiming him, "Worthy art thou", as the one who was slain and the redeemer (5:8-10). The acclamation is immediately taken up by myriads on myriads of angels, who proclaim the slain Lamb as "worthy" to receive the sevenfold attributes of "power and wealth and wisdom and might and honour and glory and blessing" (5:11-12). Glory and honour and power were attributed to God in 4:11, and when the whole chorus of creatures, angels and elders worship God again in 7:12, it is with another list of seven attributes that largely overlap with those of the Lamb: "blessing and glory and wisdom and thanksgiving and honour and power and might". The worship of God and of the Lamb is, therefore, very similar in form and in language, and so it is not surprising to find that they are worshipped together by the whole created order: "To him who sits upon the throne and to the Lamb be blessing and honour and glory and might for ever and ever" (5:13); and together acclaimed by the great multitude in heaven: "Salvation belongs to our God who sits upon the throne and to the Lamb!' (7:10). The worship of Christ the Lamb both with, and in the same terms as, God, is very striking, and John makes its implications quite clear. When he attempts, on two occasions, to fall down and worship his interpreting angel, he is told sternly, "I am a fellow servant with you ... worship God" (19:10, 22:8-9). God alone is to be worshipped; but the Lamb is also worshipped. We have already seen how in the development of his images of Christ the seer gives them a dimension in terms of the language of God; and the worship of the Lamb is entirely consistent with that imagery. It is an extraordinary fact that in the often disparaged Apocalypse of John we are given through imagery and the language of worship perhaps the "highest" Christology of the New Testament, if by that is meant a clear and consistent expression of belief in the divinity of Christ.

Christ with God is the object of worship, then; and we now turn to the identity of their worshippers. To begin with, they are the inhabitants of heaven: the four living creatures, the elders around the throne, and the myriads of angels; but subsequently other voices come to be heard. In 7:10 the acclamation of God and the Lamb together is made by the great multitude "who have come out of the great tribulation" (7:14), whom we have earlier identified as identical both with the ideal people of God, the hundred and forty-four thousand of 7:4-8, and with the Lamb's army of 14:1: the martyrs. They now join the heavenly service of worship, for "they are before the throne of God, and serve him day and night within his temple" (7:15), and they sing "a new song" which only they can learn (14:3). In 15:2-4 we are shown "those who had conquered (from) the beast and its image and the number of its name" also singing in heaven; "the conqueror" we have also seen to be one of John's distinctive terms for the martyr, and this group is clearly those who have opposed the worship of the beast, with the inevitable result. The song which they sing is identified as "the song of Moses and the song of the Lamb" (15:3).

It is somewhat surprising to find Moses introduced as a heavenly composer or choirmaster, especially as the song is not obviously related to either of the songs of Moses found in Exodus 15 and Deuteronomy 32 (unless it be that as the martyr-singers stand "beside the sea", 15:2, they recall God's victory at the Red Sea as celebrated in Exod. 15:1-10). One answer may be that there is some evidence that Deuteronomy 32, with its celebration of Israel's deliverance and Yahweh's retribution on her enemies, was drawn on in Jewish martyrology: the seven brothers and their mother, in the story of their deaths in 2 Maccabees 7, encourage each other by recalling and quoting that song of Moses (7:6; cf. Deut. 32:36). So it may be simply a convention that martyrs sing a "Moses song", even if not in Moses' words. However, another factor may be that Moses' song in Deuteronomy 32 has a second singer: Joshua (32:44), whose Greek name, as found in the Septuagint, is *Iēsous,* Jesus.

The song of Moses there is the song of "Moses and Jesus"; John's martyrs sing "the song of Moses and the song of the Lamb", the Lamb whose identity with Jesus is never in doubt since he bears the marks of the one who was slain and lives.[6]

Finally, the voice of "a great multitude in heaven" sings three triumphant Hallelujahs, celebrating the achieving of God's judgment on the great harlot and his avenging of his servants' blood, and rejoicing at the coming marriage of the Lamb (19:1-3, 6). It is reasonable to identify these voices as those of the multitude who are the martyrs who sing in 7:9-10, especially as the army of the Lamb (now seen as the rider on the white horse) reappears in 19:14.[7] On four occasions, then, the martyrs join in the worship of heaven, and theirs are the only human voices to do so. (In 5:13 God and the Lamb are honoured by "every creature in heaven and on earth and under the earth and in the sea": *pan ktisma,* the neuter noun, should be understood as denoting the created order apart from men, who manifestly do not join in paying that honour.) The martyrs, as we have seen, are supremely for John the followers and imitators of Christ; they deserve and receive especial honour and vindication because they share in his work of witness and conquest. As they alone will reign with Christ in his millennial kingdom, it is appropriate that before that time it is they alone who can join in the worship of God and the Lamb in heaven.

Thus the singers, and the object of their song; we now turn to examine the songs themselves, and their origins in terms of their form and language. Naturally, there is a good deal of influence from the language of worship in the Old Testament, though

---

[6]The coincidence of the name Joshua/Jesus is noted by the author of the epistle of Barnabas, who finds therein Joshua's rôle as a prophet of the Son of God (Barn. 12:9-10). It is surprising that there is not more development of a "Joshua-typology" in early Christian literature, considering both the name and Joshua's function as the leader under whom Israel entered in to God's promise, the land.

[7]In fact, this multitude makes the same sort of noise as the hundred and forty-four thousand of 14:2; "like the sound of many waters and the sound of mighty thunderpeals"; which is in turn like the sound of the voice of the son of man in 1:5, "like the sound of many waters". At the risk of a fanciful pun, it may be said that the martyrs "echo" Christ!

more surprisingly nothing significant from the messianic psalms 2, 8 and 110 which are widely drawn on by other early Christian writers. The song of the four living creatures in 4:8 is the *trisagion* of Isaiah's vision (Isa. 6:3); the celebration in heaven and by the twenty-four elders of the kingdom and reign of God and Christ (11:15-18) probably reflects the so-called "enthronement psalms" with their triumphant opening statement, "The Lord reigns!" (Pss. 93, 97 and 99); the identification of "new songs" in 5:9 and 4:3 may recall the introductory exhortations to "sing unto the Lord a new song" of Pss. 96 and 98; the "hallelujah choruses" of 19:1, 3, 4 and 6 certainly recall the *Hallel* psalms, 146-150, whose opening cry, "Praise the Lord!", was transliterated rather than translated in the Septuagint, *Allelouia,* as here. In two striking respects, however, the language of worship in the Apocalypse lacks biblical precedent: in its celebration of God and the Lamb through lists of their attributes, and in its characteristic form of acclamation, "Worthy art thou. . ." (4:11, 5:9, 12).

Let us look first at the pattern into which these celebrations and acclamations fall. The impression given is of antiphonal singing: choir answering choir. In chapters 4 and 5, for example, the four living creatures open with their *trisagion* to God (4:8), and the twenty-four elders respond, "Worthy art thou. . ." (vv. 9-11). These two then combine to form one choir to celebrate the Lamb's achievement in 5:8-10, to which the even mightier chorus of the myriads and myriads of angels replies with his sevenfold attributes (5:11). "All creation" follows, linking God and the Lamb together in crescendo (5:13), and finally the four living creatures return with a concluding "Amen" (5:14).[8] The impression is of a highly dramatic, highly orchestrated performance. It is not especially reminiscent of anything in biblical tradition, but it is strongly evocative of the Hellenistic theatre: of the rôle of the chorus in drama, commenting on and explaining the action, and particularly of the choral performances of the *ōdeion.* Nor were such choral performances confined to the

---

[8]Antiphonal singing is also found in 7:9-12, 11:15-18, 16:5-7 and 19:1-8.

setting of the theatre: they would take place at festivals, games and horse-races.[9] In particular, they would be a feature of the Imperial cult. At festivals in the emperor's honour, where his statue might dominate the celebration, there would be games, sacrifices, processions and "competitions in music and poetry, for which the emperor's greatness would be the theme."[10] In fact, there were special functionaries of the cult called *humnōdoi*, whose activity was centred in Asia Minor and in Ephesus in particular, and whose task it was to compose such songs and choruses in the emperor's honour. We have no record of their productions, occasional pieces as they must have been, but it is reasonable to suppose that the celebration of such imperial attributes as "power and wealth and wisdom and might and glory and honour and blessing" would not have been alien to them. Scott gives examples of the terms in which the court poets Martial and Statius habitually celebrated Domitian as victor and invincible, especially in his character as Jupiter, and as peacemaker; they spoke of his "radiance", and they applied to him epithets such as *maximus, magnus* and *tantus*.[11] Other scholars have claimed that the Apocalypse's distinctive form of acclamation, "Worthy art thou!", has parallels in the poetry and song of the imperial cult: "Among them [i.e., forms of acclamation mentioned by court poets and other writers which probably go back to the time of Domitian] were the following: Hail, Victory, Lord of the Earth, Invincible, Power, Glory, Honour, Peace, Security, Holy, Blessed, Great, Unequalled, Thou Alone, Worthy art Thou, Worthy is he to inherit the Kingdom...", but the claim falls short of definite proof.[12]

---

[9] A similar comparison is made by G. Delling, *Worship in the New Testament,* London, 1962, pp. 83f.

[10] G.W. Bowersock, "The Imperial Cult: Perceptions and Persistence" in B.E. Meyer and E.P. Sanders, *Jewish and Christian Self-Definition,* vol. 3, London, 1982, p. 173.

[11] *The Imperial Cult under the Flavians,* pp. 92, 94f., 116f.

[12] E. Stauffer, *Christ and the Caesars,* London, 1955, p. 155; cf. E. Peterson, *Heis Theos,* Göttingen, 1926, pp. 176-179. Unfortunately Stauffer deliberately declined to provide any footnotes from which his references might be checked, while Peterson does not offer any evidence contemporary with the Apocalypse.

We may not, therefore, be able to tie the threads as tightly as we might wish, but we may suggest that here again the presentation of worship relates to a major theme in the Apocalypse. The author expects conflict between the Christian churches and the power of Rome: he sees this conflict as one of rival claims, and as focussed on the demand of the beast for worship, and he interprets it through imagery and parody. Those, now, who enter into John's vision of the worship of heaven may make an imaginative contrast with experience in their own world. They see "him who sits upon the throne", with the Lamb at his side, bearing that evocative title "our Lord and God" (4:11),[13] greeted with prostration, *proskunēsis* (4:10, 5:8, 7:11, 19:4; this characteristic act of obeisance to the divine ruler passed from the oriental into the Hellenistic world from the time of Alexander onwards); presented with golden crowns (4:4,10: "a ceremony inherited by the Romans from the traditions of hellenistic kingship");[14] and celebrated in mighty choruses which in their form and content would strike chords familiar in the Asian cities. The Christians in those cities can participate in an "imperial cult" of their own, directed to its proper object. As with his development of the images of the adversaries, so John's presentation of heavenly worship has a strongly polemical edge, and here its impact comes through counter-parody: as the beast falsely claimed the status and character of the Lamb, so now the Lamb truly claims and gives content to the beast's own forms of worship.[15]

[13]See p. 72.

[14]D. Aune, "The Influence of Roman Court Ceremonial on the Apocalypse of John", *Biblical Research* 28, 1983, p. 12; Aune draws similar comparisons between John's vision and the imperial court and cult.

[15]One final comment on this line of argument may be allowed: the author of the Apocalypse is traditionally known as John "the Theologian". We do not know the origin of the title; it is explained by fourth-century Fathers like Gregory of Nazianzus as due to his primacy (as being also the author of the Fourth Gospel) in expounding the doctrine of the Logos. However, the term *theologos,* god-speaker, was another term for the *hymnōdi* of the imperial cult (thus Deissmann, *Light,* pp. 348f., and Carnegie, *art. cit.,* p. 254, n. 45). If John is indeed translating the imperial worship into the songs of the Lamb, it is a most appropriate title for him.

To conclude, then; worship is an integral part of the vision of the Apocalypse: integral not only in that it is so marked a feature of the book, but in that it serves to illustrate and expound its major themes of the character of Christ, the rôle of the martyrs, and the conflict with the beast. We may, however, raise one outstanding question. The worship of the Apocalypse is clearly in its content and its setting "Christian worship", but what is its relation to the Christian worship actually practiced at the time? We have considered its derivation from the biblical language of worship and from the worship of the Hellenistic world, and we should at least consider the possibility that it may also have roots in the churches which John addresses.

The worship of the Apocalypse is to a very large extent worship by singing, and it is clear that singing played a part in the life of the New Testament communities. Paul and Silas sing hymns in their jail at Philippi, with the other prisoners listening (Acts 16:25); James advocates singing when cheerful (Jas. 5:13); Paul indicates that someone might contribute a hymn during the church's meeting, as another might contribute speech in tongues or interpretation (1 Cor. 14:26), and he encourages the Colossian Christians to "sing psalms and hymns and spiritual songs with thankfulness in your hearts to God" (Col. 3:16, cf. also Eph. 5:19).[16] The Christians interrogated by Pliny, ca. A.D. 112, describe how "they were accustomed to meet together on a fixed day before dawn and to sing a hymn in alternate parts to Christ as a god" (*Epistula* X.96.7). It is, however, difficult to establish the content of these Christian songs. Some scholars identify "Christological hymns" in the New Testament, such as Phil. 2:6-11, Col. 1:15-20, Eph. 2:14-16, 1 Tim. 3:16, 1 Pet. 3:18-22, Heb. 1:3, and maybe also the Johannine "prologue", John 1:1-18, at least in its original core.[17] James Dunn suggests

---

[16]It is not clear whether the adjective "spiritual" qualifies all three nouns, so that all Chrisian singing is seen as part of their experience of life in the Spirit, or whether the last, "spiritual songs", is singing in tongues, as in the contrast between singing "with the spirit" and "with the mind" in 1 Cor. 14:15; the latter view is taken by J.D.G. Dunn, *Jesus and the Spirit,* London, 1975, pp. 238f.

[17]These passages are discussed, with a survey of scholarly investigation into New Testament hymnody, by J.T. Sanders, *The New Testament Christological Hymns,* Cambridge, 1971.

that doxologies like Rom. 11:33-36, Phil. 4:20, and 1 Tim. 1:17 might be "utterances typical of the cries which must have punctuated the worship of the Pauline assemblies."[18] The four "canticles" of the opening chapters of Luke's gospel, the *Magnificat* (1:46-55), *Benedictus* (1:68-79), *Gloria* (2:14) and *Nunc Dimittis* (2:29-35) might also have been, or become, the hymns of a particular Christian community, perhaps of the Palestinian church. Christological hymns which celebrate the kerygma, the saving event of Christ, would find a parallel in Rev. 5:9-10, and doxologies, giving glory to God, would find theirs in Rev. 5:13 and 7:12; and thus John might be seen to draw upon the hymns of the churches for his songs of the Lamb.

It may be, then, that when John's readers heard his account of the worship of heaven they found that it harmonized with their own worship on earth. But we must enter two caveats. First, there is that difficulty in identifying the other hymns from which to draw the parallels: there are no firmly established criteria for distinguishing in a New Testament document between an originally independent "hymn" and a prayer, a creed or confession, non-hymnic poetry, or indeed the author's own elevated prose. Secondly, the worship of Revelation is precisely the worship of heaven, or of the cosmos in 5:13, and not that of men on earth; and it is what John sees, or rather hears, in his vision. This must give us pause, for conclusions about his sources involve judgments on his character. He may be a highly conscious and deliberate writer, drawing upon what he knows and interpreting it to maximum effect; or he may be an imaginative artist, freely creating his own effects (and maybe himself the creator of that distinctive "Worthy art thou" form); or he may be primarily the prophet, so that our emphasis should be more on what he is "given" than on what he "has". It is with the assessment of John as Christian prophet that our next, and final, chapter will be concerned.

[18]*Op. cit.*, p. 239. We might add to his list Jude 24-25.

6

The Christian Prophecy

In the introduction to my opening chapter I indicated something of the sharp division of opinion which the Apocalypse has provoked in Christian history. In twentieth century scholarship, however, it has evoked one notable and unwonted agreement: between Rudolf Bultmann, usually stigmatized as the epitome of the "German radical", and C.H. Dodd, similarly regarded as the great representative of "English conservatism". Bultmann describes the Revelation of John as "a weakly Christianized Judaism", its eschatology that of the Jewish apocalypses rather than the distinctive Christian hope,[1] while Dodd, discussing it in the context of distinguishing between prophecy and apocalyptic, judges it "only superficially Christian".[2]

These judgments may serve as the text for this final chapter, since the argument throughout has been that so far from being "superficially Christian", the centrality of Christ in the author's mind has led him to develop, indeed to transform, inherited ideas and images. His characteristic image of Christ is, of course, "the Lamb", but it is worth noting how frequently the simple personal name "Jesus" is used: John's apocalypse is "the revelation of Jesus Christ" (1:1), and his testimony is "the testimony of Jesus" (19:10), because "I Jesus have sent my angel to you" (22:16); the martyrs whom he values so highly are "the martyrs

---

[1] *Theology of the New Testament,* vol. 2, p. 175. We have already found reason to disagree with Bultmann's argument, p. 65, n. 17.

[2] *The Authority of the Bible,* revised edition, London, 1960, p. 180.

of Jesus" (17:6); and his closing prayer is "Come, Lord Jesus!" (22:10). My thesis has been that his consciousness of what we have called "the facts of Jesus", the central Christian preaching of his death and resurrection, has led the author to develop and extend traditional Messianic imagery; to present the great adversary of the Christ in his character as a parody of the Lamb, and thus to show the essence of the conflict expected between their followers; to re-evaluate the experience of martyrdom, and in so doing to give a new content to the hope of the millennial kingdom; and that all these developments find expression in the language of worship that is so much a feature of his vision.

At the risk of building too far upon a house of cards, the parody theme expounded in chapter three might be elaborated to explain two elements in the image of the adversaries that were there glossed over. First, the war against the saints of chapter 13 is launched not by one beast but by two: the beast from the sea (13:1) and the beast from the land (13:11). This second beast acts in relation to the first, exercising his authority and enforcing his worship (13:12-15); and he also appears as "the false prophet" (16:13, 19:20). A common theory is that this double image reflects the twofold experience of Roman power, as exercised "from the sea" with authority from Rome itself (as by the proconsul of Asia), and as exercised "from the land" by the indigenous authorities, and expecially the eager proponents of the imperial cult in Asia Minor. The experience of Roman power, however, hardly requires such a nice distinction about its origins, and the development of the images may have more to do with the Christian experience of power: the dragon, beast and beast-prophet standing as an unholy trinity in opposition to God, Christ and the Spirit. It must be admitted that there is not a great deal of reference to the Spirit in the Apocalypse of John apart from the three-fold greeting in its introduction from "him who is and who was and who is to come, and from the seven spirits who are before his throne, and from Jesus Christ" (1:4-5, the "seven spirits" are seen before the throne in 4:5), but what there is said relates the Spirit to Christ in analogy with the relation of the second beast to the first. As the second beast acts for the first and exercises his authority (13:12), so the "seven spirits" are under the authority of the one like a son of man (3:1, cf. 1:22), and the "seven spirits of God sent out into all the earth" are the eyes of the Lamb (5:6). Again, as the second beast enables the image of the first to speak (13:15) and appears later as "the false prophet", so the Spirit is the inspirer of true prophecy: John is "in the Spirit" when he receives his vision (1:10) and the messages that he conveys to the seven churches from the one like a son of man are also identified as "what the Spirit says to the churches" (2:7, 11, 17, 29, 3:6, 13, 22; cf. the suggestive but epigrammatic comment that "the testimony of Jesus is the spirit of prophecy", 19:10).

Secondly, our discussion of the images of the beast of chapter 13 and the harlot of chapter 17 treated them as both images of persecuting Rome, the inheritor of the legacy of wicked empires and wicked cities.[3] They might therefore seem to be alternative and interchangeable images, yet in 17:3 they are found together, with the harlot riding on the beast's back. It has been suggested that the images are given an independent life as pointing respectively to Rome's political and economic power, but again such a distinction is unnecessary and based on modern category distinctions which John is unlikely to have made. The explanation, again, more plausibly lies in John's parody motif: the Lamb has a bride "clothed in fine linen, pure and bright" (19:7-8), who is also the holy city (21:2, 9-11); it is congruous with this that the beast whose evil is expressed in his parody of the good should be united not with a pure bride but with a promiscuous and drunken harlot (18:9, 17:6), who is also the unholy city of blood (18:24). The two images of the beast and the harlot are given their independent life under the influence of the Christian concepts of Christ and his Church. We are not, of course, dealing with the rationalization of theological argument but with the expression in imagery of Christian intuition and experience. The experience of power as the power of the Spirit of God and the apprehension of the close and necessary relationship between Christ and his community is conveyed not only through the imagery for the Christian realities themselves but of what is seen to stand over against them: hostile and ultimately demonic

[3]See above, pp. 36-37.

power that is allied to and expressed in human societies.

We would, then, firmly reject the description of the Revelation of John as "weakly Christianized"; but what of the other side of our scholars' argument, that it is to be addressed primarily as an apocalypse? John it was who gave that genre of literature its name, and in our first chapter we discussed the characteristics of the book that lead it to be classified within the genre: its conviction of imminent divine intervention; its universal perspective; its "two-dimensional" vision of events on earth having their heavenly parallel; and its copious use of imagery and cryptic symbol. Yet though the Revelation belongs as literature unmistakably to the apocalyptic genre, we would suggest that some of those characteristic features of it take on a new emphasis because this is a *Christian* apocalypse.

First we may consider that vision of events as having two dimensions, earthly and heavenly. The traditional hope of apocalyptic is of the resolution of earthly conflict, impossible in human terms, because there is strength in heaven: thus in Daniel 10 and 12 it is the angelic champions of Israel who will ensure her victory over the Syrian oppressor, and in the *War Rule* of Qumran the angelic "sons of light" will ensure the victory of the sons of light in Israel over the "sons of darkness" whose earthly manifestation is the power of occupying Rome. So in Revelation 5 it is in heaven that the Lamb appears, to open the sealed book and put into action the final plan of God; but in v. 9 he is said to be worthy to do so because he was "slaughtered": the decisive event is thus the earthly one, of his death. Similarly in 12:7-12 there is war "in heaven" between Michael and the angelic army and the army of the dragon, but the victory of the former is gained, in v. 11, "by the blood of the Lamb and by the word of their testimony, for they loved not their lives even unto death": the earthly events of the deaths of Jesus and his martyrs who follow him. The two dimensions remain, but the balance of power has shifted so that it is the paradoxical "strength in weakness" of the Lamb's death that ensures the resolution of conflict not only on earth but also in heaven.

Secondly, the traditional apocalyptic vision includes the idea of entities which are kept now in heaven, to descend at the new age whose dawn is imminent; and thus John too sees the new

Jerusalem which has been prepared descending to be the dwelling of God with men in the new heaven and new earth (21:2, 10). In 1 Enoch the "son of man" himself is being kept in heaven for his future revelation in the new age (1 Enoch 62, especially v. 7). John, too, sees Christ as the Lamb in heaven in 5:6 and, as the rider on the white horse, coming from the opened heaven as the executor of the final judgment of God (19:11-16). However, he also sees him as the "one like a son of man" who holds in his hand the seven stars (1:16); the "angels" of the seven churches, which are themselves symbolized by the seven lampstands (v. 20). We have already noted how the author here translates the idea of nations having their individual angelic or heavenly authorities so that it now relates to the character of the Church, while the nation of Rome has as its heavenly authority no angel but the great cosmic adversary of God, the dragon.[4] In the present context what is important is that although the son of man "holds" the stars, he "walks" among the lampstands. He controls the angelic guardians, but he is present not with them in heaven but among the churches on earth. For the seer of the Christian apocalypse, his Christ is not a figure kept in heaven to be awaited at the end of time: Christ the Lamb is indeed in the present exalted in heaven, but he is so exalted because he has already come to earth, and died; Christ the rider on the white horse will certainly come in the future to act as the judge, but he is already experienced as the son of man active among the churches. That tension between realized hope and future expectation, the "already" and the "not yet" found in the preaching of Jesus and elsewhere in the New Testament is found here too.

One further difference from the traditional genre also deserves note. In other apocalyptic literature the author takes his stand in the past. He assumes the identity of a past figure: he is Daniel, Ezra or Baruch from the time of Israel's exile, or Enoch or Joseph in the patriarchal age. From that standpoint he surveys and interprets through his symbols the course of what is in fact to him past history, up to his own real present, and then projects his vision into the future (e.g., Daniel 8 and 11, and cf.

Enoch's account of the fortunes of bulls and sheep, 1 Enoch 85-90). The seer of Revelation, by contrast, assumes no past identity, but addresses his readers as their contemporary: "I, John, your brother and partaker with you in tribulation" (1:9).[5] He provides no survey of the past; although we have shown how Rome in her character as the "great city" is described in terms of Babylon, Tyre, Sodom, Egypt and Jerusalem, this was to describe her as cumulatively the inheritor of their character and not to give a chronicle of her predecessors. Consistently with all this, too, whereas in other apocalypses the author is told to "seal" his book for the time to come (Dan. 12:9), John is told to leave his unsealed, "for the time is near" (22:10). He addresses himself, then, directly and immediately to the situation in which he is himself expressly involved.

It is a nice irony that although it is the author of Revelation who gave to the genre of apocalyptic its name, his own convictions cannot be expressed precisely in its traditional terms and so these have been adapted to his purpose. The content of his message has controlled its form, rather than the reverse.[6] So we may turn to another way in which his work may be classified. He may have characterized it in its opening as "apocalypse", but his most frequent term for it is "prophecy": thus 1:3, 10:11, 22:7, 10, 18 and 19. His claims for his prophecy are large: "blessed is he who reads aloud the words of the prophecy, and blessed are those who hear, and who keep what is written therein" (1:3); and by contrast there is a curse on anyone who adds to or subtracts from it (22:18f.). However, John does not see himself as the only

---

[5]It is sometimes argued that Revelation differs from traditional apocalyptic in that its authorship is "not pseudonymous" (thus B. W. Jones, "More about the Apocalypse as Apocalyptic," *J.B.L.* 87, 1968, pp. 325-7); but there is in fact no formal difference between a vision given to "I, John" and one to "I, Daniel" or "I, Enoch," and "John" could equally be a pseudonym, adopted perhaps by a disciple of the apostle. The real difference lies in this author's addressing his real contemporaries and their situation directly, rather than speaking to them as a prophet from their past—a difference that may indeed make pseudonymous authorship improbable.

[6]For the relation of this view of the Apocalypse of John to the appeal to apocalyptic in contemporary systematic theology, especially that of Wolfhart Pannenberg, see Sophie Laws, "Can Apocalyptic Be Relevant?" in *What about the New Testament?*, Essays in Honour of Christopher Evans, edited by Morna Hooker and Colin Hickling, London, 1975, pp.89-102.

or exclusive prophet of his day: his "brethren" the prophets are spoken of in 22:9, and prophets as a group are also referred to in 10:7, 11:18, 16:6, 18:20, 24 and 22:6, as also "that woman Jezebel, who calls herself a prophet"[7] in Thyatira is castigated in 2:20. Prophets are associated with martyrdom in 16:4 and 18:24, and correspondingly the two figures who symbolize the martyrs' witness in chapter 11 are also said to prophesy (11:3, 10). The image of the prophet as the martyr is not new with John, but has precedent in Jewish tradition about the fates of Jeremiah, Isaiah, Ezekiel and others, as reflected in Jesus' reference to the blood of the prophets (Matt. 23:34f. and Lk. 11:49-51) and to their perishing in Jerusalem (Lk. 13:33).[8] It is, however, consistent with John's estimation of both martyrdom and prophecy that he should associate the two: not all martyrs are prophets, but prophets are prominent among the martyrs.

Prophecy was clearly part of the experience of earliest Christianity. As well as from the Apocalypse, we have evidence in the New Testament from Paul, who contrasts it favourably with the gift of tongues (1 Cor. 14), and from Acts, in the figures of Agabus (11:28, 21:10f.) and the four daughters of Philip (21:8-9) and in a group at Antioch which, according to Luke, included Paul himself (13:1f.). Among the early Christian writings known collectively as "the Apostolic Fathers", the *Didache* gives instruction about itinerant prophets (chapters 11 and 13) and Hermas supplies guidance for testing true and false prophets (*Mandate* 11). The middle to late second century saw a re-

---

[7]It is worth noting *en passant* that the Greek word *prophētēs* has no variation for masculine and feminine endings, so the RSV's description of Jezebel as a "prophetess" rather than a "prophet" is unnecessary, if not actually misleading, as is the description of Phoebe of Cenchreae as a "deaconess" rather than a "deacon" in Rom. 16:1.

[8]In the Old Testament the only prophets to meet violent death are Zechariah the son of Jehoiada (2 Chron. 24:20-22; cf. Matt. 23:35) and Uriah the son of Shemaiah (Jer. 26:20-23), but an account of Isaiah's death is given in the *Ascension of Isaiah* 1-5, and for references to the martyrdoms of Ezekiel and Zechariah, see M. R. James, *The Lost Apocrypha of the Old Testament,* London, 1920, pp. 68f. and 75. For a discussion of the tradition of prophets' martyrdom as it is reflected in the New Testament, see also G. W. H. Lampe, "Martyrdom and Inspiration," in W. Horbury and B. McNeil, eds., *Suffering and Martyrdom in the New Testament,* especially pp. 123-129.

surgence of the phenomenon in a movement called "Montanism" after its founder and leader, or "the New Prophecy", after its dominant characteristic.[9]

Montanus and his two women followers, Priscilla and Maximilla, began to prophesy in Phrygia, and they attracted a popular following which spread from Asia Minor to Gaul and Africa, to include the great thinker and polemicist Tertullian and, according to him, almost won the recognition of the bishop of Rome (*Adversus Praxeas* 1.4f.). Yet Montanism was ultimately condemned, its followers excommunicated in Asia and forced into schism in Africa. Various accusations were levelled against it, catalogued in Eusebius's account. Its leaders were accused of decadence and immorality: "Does a prophet paint his eyelids?... Does a prophet play at gaming-tables and dice?" (*H.E.*V.18.11);[10] and of money-grubbing, because the leaders were paid (18.2b,4); though also, and inconsistently, for asceticism (18.2a-3). It was alleged that, in an age of increasing pressure upon Christians, the Montanists did not produce martyrs (16.20-21); this was probably simply untrue, for Tertullian quotes a prophecy encouraging a desire for death in martyrdom rather than by illness, childbirth or in bed,[11] and the *Passion of Perpetua* indicates that she, one of the most revered, and certainly one of the most sympathetic and attractive, of early Christian martyrs, was a Montanist believer.[12] They were attacked for the failure of their prophecies of the imminent

---

[9] Eusebius' description of Montanism is heavily dependent upon the hostile accounts of Apollonius and an anonymous author (*H. E.* V. 16-19); utterances of Montanist prophets may be found collected in E. Hennecke, *New Testament Apocrypha* II, pp. 685-689, and a discussion of the history of Montanism (including the question of its date) in T. D. Barnes, *Tertullian,* Oxford, 1971, pp. 82-84, 130-142 and 253-254.

[10] These accusations sound like simple abuse, though it was suggested by a member of the audience, Dr. John Spencer, that the "dicing" might have been the casting of lots as a means of prophetic divination.

[11] *De Fuga* 9.4, quoted in Hennecke, p. 687.

[12] For text and translation of the *Passion of Perpetua,* see Herbert Musurillo,S. J., *The Acts of the Christian Martyrs,* Oxford, 1972, pp. 106-131. For indications of its, and her, Montanist sympathies, see sections 1.1-5 and 21.11 and the discussion by Barnes, *Tertullian,* pp. 71-79.

descent of the New Jerusalem upon Pepuza in Phrygia (16.18-
19, 18.2),[13] but probably the most substantial accusation against
them was not that their prophecies failed, but that they were not
authentic Christian prophecy at all: the Montanists prophesied
"contrary to the manner which the Church had received from
generation to generation by tradition from the beginning"
(16.7b); "they cannot show any prophet under either the Old or
New [covenant] who was moved by the Spirit after this manner"
(16.3).

Montanism, "the New Prophecy", therefore raises the question
of what early Christian prophecy was like, and of whether we
can establish from the New Testament a clear picture of the
Christian prophet's distinctive rôle and mode of action in the
light of which we could assess subsequent claimants to it.[14] Paul,
in 1 Cor. 14, may provide us with an initial sketch. He regards
prophecy, obviously, as a gift of the Spirit (14:1, cf. 12:10), but,
unlike tongues, it is a gift of speech that is in itself intelligible
communication, that "speaks to men" with no need for interpretation (14:2-3). It is human speech, and it is a gift which is not
essentially private but which is exercised within, and for, the
church; it "edifies the church" (14:4). It may also, however, serve
to communicate to unbelievers, bringing them to respond as
tongues cannot (14:23-25). However, in order that the gift may
be of greatest benefit to the church, it should be, like tongues,
regulated; and it can be, because "the spirits of prophets are
subject to prophets" (14:29-32). Despite the injunction of 14:34f.,
requiring women to keep silent in the churches, it is clear from
11:5 that women as well as men might prophesy; presumably if

[13]The passages in Eusebius allude to utterances of Montanus and Maximilla;
Epiphanius quotes a specific prophecy from Priscilla, *Haereses* 49.1.2-3, quoted in
Hennecke, p. 687. The Montanists' millenarianism would not, of course, of itself put
them out of step with second-century Christianity.

[14]Prophecy in the New Testament has recently been the subject of much discussion,
raised in part no doubt by the charismatic movement in major Christian denominations
which often includes what is claimed to be prophetic speech. Studies include D. Hill,
New Testament Prophecy, Atlanta, Georgia, 1979; D. E. Aune, *Prophecy in Early
Christianity and the Ancient Mediterranean World*, Grand Rapids, Mich., 1983, and J.
D. G. Dunn, *Jesus and the Spirit*, pp. 170-176, 227-233.

their speech was a gift from the Spirit they might utter it. Yet Paul's evidence is very limited. As with the gift of tongues, he does not set out to describe an experience with which both he and his readers are familiar; nor is prophecy in fact his object of concern: he only writes about it in order to show up the contrast with tongues, to commend it over against tongues, and thus to put the Corinthians' enthusiasm for this latter gift into proportion. In particular, Paul does not help us to answer the very important question of the content of early Christian prophecy: prophecy, he insists, is communication; but what did the prophet say? Paul's only indication of an answer is couched in the most general possible terms: the prophet speaks "upbuilding and encouragement and consolation" (14:3); "all may learn and all be encouraged" (14:31); while in relation to unbelievers the word may also have a judging effect (14:24f.). This, tantalizingly, does not take us very far.

We may turn, then, to a second source of information: that of Acts. From Luke's account of the prophetic group at Antioch, of Agabus and of the daughters of Philip, we might deduce a number of characteristics of earliest Christian prophecy. First, the prophet speaks in the name of the Holy Spirit: thus Agabus (Acts 21:11) and the reported words of the Holy Spirit to, and surely through, the Antiochene group (13:2). The speech contains direction: the sending out of Paul and Barnabas (13:2f.); and prediction: Agabus's prophecies of the universal famine (11:28) and of the arrest of Paul (the message given in words and in symbolic action, 21:10-11). Then, as with Paul, prophecy is seen as operating within the church, in the group within the church of Antioch; and Luke's reference to the four unmarried daughters of Philip (21:8-9, one may have a certain sympathy for the father of that household!) shows that Luke, like Paul, assumed that both men and women might be prophets.

Yet there are two major difficulties in using Luke's evidence to establish a norm. First, he expressly includes Paul himself among the prophets of Antioch. This raises the question of how much of Paul's activity Luke would see as "prophetic" so that we might extrapolate from it to fill out his picture; quite apart from the question of whether Paul would have accepted this characterization (he reminds the Corinthians that he possesses the gift of tongues, but it is not obvious that he enjoys the "higher gift" of prophecy, 1 Cor. 14:18f.). Secondly, Luke sees the Pentecost experience (Acts 2:1-13) as a fulfilment of Joel's prediction of God's gift of prophecy in the last days (2:16-22, quoting Joel 2:28-32). The experience of Pentecost was, according to Luke, of miraculously given speech, "other tongues" (2:4), which he describes as a means of communication in a variety of languages: "we hear, each of us in his own native language" (2:8, cf. 2:6, 11). Yet Luke also reports that the Pentecost gift was mocked as the incoherent speech of drunkenness (2:13, 15). It may be that Luke has conflated the two spiritual gifts of speech, tongues and prophecy, which Paul kept carefully distinct, and we may wonder whether he, like Paul, had a personal knowledge of the two to enable him to keep them distinct;[15] certainly it would only be with great caution that we could use his account of Pentecost in building up our picture of Christian prophecy.

In the somewhat limited light of all this, we may turn back to the Apocalypse of John as a third possible source of evidence. It would, of course, give us much more information about the content of Christian prophecy. The seer is obviously very much concerned with predicting the imminent future, and is thus broadly similar to Agabus in Acts. Yet he is also very much concerned, as we have stressed, with interpreting the present, and with showing the true nature of the situation in which conflict and crisis will arise. In the seven letters his concern is with the immediate and direct guidance of the churches, with encouragement, warning and judgment; thus Smyrna is encouraged (2:10), Sardis warned (3:2-3), and Laodicea judged (3:15-19). Again, broadly speaking, this is consistent with Paul's definition of the content of prophecy in 1 Cor. 14:3. It may also be noted that John, like Luke and Paul, assumes that women as well as men may prophesy: his quarrel with "that woman

---

[15]Other explanations of Luke's account are, of course, possible. A number of people speaking at the same time in different languages may well produce a confused babble; alternatively tongue-speaking by some may have been accompanied by a simultaneous gift of interpretation to others; and charismatic groups have often claimed that speaking in tongues is the use of rare languages whose identity is revealed by the chance presence of a native speaker in the group where the phenomenon occurs.

Jezebel" (2:20) and his rejection of her claim to prophetic authority is a matter of her message, not her sex.

He also tells us more about the reception of the prophetic message. John receives his testimony in visionary experience: he is "in the Spirit on the Lord's day" (1:10) when he sees the one like a son of man and is given the messages for the churches, and he is taken up "in the Spirit" to heaven to be shown "what must take place after this" (4:1-2). This may be the record of ecstatic experience like that of Paul, who was "caught up into Paradise—whether in the body or out of the body I do not know" and heard "things that cannot be told, which man may not utter" (2 Cor. 12:1-4). John certainly sees the unseeable or unimaginable, like the Lamb "standing as slaughtered" (5:6), but he can tell of what he sees, and his account of his vision is very conscious, very controlled; we have argued that there is a discernible structure to it and that images and ideas interrelate to considerable effect. The visionary context for John's message could be seen as the employment of a literary convention, or as the work of artistic creation; if, however, it is regarded as authentic prophetic vision then the spirit of this prophet is certainly subject to the mind of the prophet.

He speaks, though, like the prophets of Acts and of Paul's experience, under divine direction. At the opening of the book there appears to be a chain of transmission: the revelation is given by God to Jesus Christ, who sent his angel to John, who then bore witness (1:1-2); but this bears little relation to the way in which the message is subsequently conveyed. The angelic interpreter plays no part until chapter 17:1, and not very much thereafter (he is identified as one of the bearers of the bowls of wrath, and his rôle is confined to the final stages of the vision, concerned with the judgment and the new age beyond it: 19:9-10, 21:9-17, 22:1-6, 22:8-11, and cf. above p. 83-84). The words which John reports are occasionally ascribed to "he who sat upon the throne" (21:5-6, cf. 1:8), but for the most part the voice which is heard directly in the prophecy is that of Jesus, the risen, exalted and present Lord. This is clear throughout the letters to the seven churches, where the "I" who addresses them is the one like a son of man of the opening vision, identified as such by his attributes in that vision (2:1, cf. 1:13, 16a; 2:12, cf. 1:16b; 2:18, cf.

1:14-15; 3:1, cf. 1:16a and also 5:6; probably also 3:7, cf. 1:18b) and in his character as the risen Jesus, "the first and the last, who died and came to life" (2:8, cf. 1:17-18), "the faithful and true witness, the beginning of God's creation" (3:14, cf. 1:5). The final promises, "I am coming soon," are also those of Jesus, as John's closing prayer confirms (22:7, 12, 20). If this prophet speaks "the word of the Lord," that Lord is most characteristically the Christian risen Lord, who takes on the rôle of the Lord God Yahweh in revealing "his secret to his servants the prophets" (Amos 3:7). Thus another feature of the Apocalypse is seen "in the light of the Lamb"; as with the address of worship to the Lamb, so the attribution to him of the words of prophecy is a significant element in the author's christology.

One further comment may be added on this last point. In the heyday of form-critical analysis of the synoptic gospels it was often argued, or assumed, that words of the exalted Jesus spoken through Christian prophets may have been absorbed without differentiation into the tradition of the teaching of Jesus during his ministry; the words were, after all, words of the same Jesus, and it would hardly have seemed necessary to the earliest Christian preachers and believers to discriminate between them. More recently, in the course of the current interest in early Christian prophecy, attempts have been made to analyse the extent to which prophets may have influenced the tradition, and to establish criteria for recognizing prophetic sayings in the synoptic gospels ("prophetic sayings," that is, which are not attributable to Jesus himself in his character as prophet!).[16] Our brief survey of the Apocalypse as prophecy may make some contribution to this discussion.

---

[16]The primary assumption is associated with the work of Rudolf Bultmann, e. g. in his *Form Criticism,* New York, 1962, pp. 52, 56. Recent discussions include J. D. G. Dunn, "Prophetic 'I'-Sayings and the Jesus tradition: The Importance of Testing Prophetic Utterances within Early Christianity," *N.T.S.* 24, 1977-78, pp. 175-198; D. Hill, *New Testament Prophecy,* pp. 160-185; D.Aune, *Prophecy in Early Christianity,* pp. 233-245. A useful survey is provided by M. E. Boring, "Christian Prophecy and the Sayings of Jesus: the State of the Question," *N.T.S.* 29, 1982-83, pp. 104-112, elaborated in his *Sayings of the Risen Jesus: Christian Prophecy in the Synoptic Tradition,* Cambridge, 1982.

First, the words of the Lord which John the prophet reports are specifically those of the risen and exalted Jesus; there is no suggestion that they are recalled from or related to the past. Secondly, there is not much resemblance between these prophetic words and material in the synoptic tradition. The isolated utterance, "Lo, I am coming like a thief! Blessed is he who is awake, keeping his garments that he may not go naked and be seen exposed!" (16:15) and the warning to the church in Sardis that "If you are not awake, I will come like a thief, and you will not know at what hour I will come upon you" (3:3) are similar in their imagery to the brief parable that "if the householder had known at what hour the thief was coming, he would have been awake and would not have left his house to be broken into" (Lk 12:39), which is similarly applied in the gospel to the coming of the Son of man. The immediately preceding section of Luke's gospel, urging "be like men who are waiting for their master to come home from the marriage feast, so that they may open to him at once when he comes and knocks. Blessed are those servants whom the master finds awake when he comes; truly, I say to you, he will gird himself and have them sit at table, and he will come and serve them" (12:36-37), has also some similarity to the assurance to the church in Laodicea that "I stand at the door and knock; if anyone hears my voice and opens the door, I will come in to him and eat with him, and he with me" (3:20). It is possible in these instances that prophetic words may have been drawn into the gospel tradition, but it is at least as possible that the remembered parables of Jesus were part of the prophet's consciousness and may have influenced the way in which he gave words to his message. Either way, the lack of any widespread similarity between the prophetic speech of the Apocalypse and the gospel material, and the very clear consciousness of this prophet that the one who speaks to him is the risen Lord, may give cause to doubt whether the words of Christian prophets would have been absorbed either very readily or very extensively among the remembered words of Jesus.[17]

---

[17]On the contribution of Revelation to the general discussion of Christian prophecy and the tradition of Jesus' teaching, see also D. Hill, "On the evidence for the creative rôle of Christian prophets," *N.T.S.* 20, 1973-74, pp. 262-274.

There are, then, broad similarities between the Apocalypse understood as prophecy and other presentations of Christian prophecy in the New Testament; it would provide, of course, considerably more material for a reconstruction of the phenomenon, and first-hand material, as actually the word of a prophet rather than the evidence of a respectful witness like Luke or Paul. However, there are difficulties in taking the Apocalypse as a paradigm of early Christian prophecy. First, although John assumes, as we have seen, that he is not unique in being a prophet, and that there are other, perhaps many other prophets, yet he assumes a certain primacy of authority. His work is sacrosanct: no addition, no subtraction; there is no impression that he, like the prophets of Luke and Paul, is subject to the judgment of the churches—quite the reverse.[18] Secondly, his prophecy is written. This does not necessarily set it apart, for there may have been other prophets who committed their word to writing but whose work has not survived. The New Testament must always be read as selective and incomplete evidence for earliest Christianity. It may mean, though, that some characteristics of John's work are strictly literary rather than prophetic, stemming from the reflective committing of his vision to writing rather than from the experience of the vision itself. We have argued that the Revelation of John, in its content, transcends the literary genre of apocalyptic, yet it is to that genre that it, as literature, belongs. Justin Martyr and Irenaeus, John's early readers, unambiguously received his work as prophecy,[19] and it is as Christian prophecy, on its own evaluation, that it must continue to be assessed; not, however, as the norm, but as one example of a varied phenomenon.

We came into this discussion by way of Montanism, and the accusation levelled against that "New Prophecy" that it was not authentic Christian prophecy in the mould of earliest Christianity, and we may pause briefly to consider the implications of our discussion for a verdict on Montanism. The

---

[18]John's assumption of a primacy of authority is also stressed by D. Hill, *ibid.* and "Prophecy and Prophets in the Revelation of St. John," *N.T.S.* 18, 1971-72, pp. 401-4.

[19]Thus Justin, *Dialogue* 81.4; Irenaeus, *Adv. Haer.* V. 30.3.

activity of women prophets would be consistent with the three New Testament sources. The predictive, indeed millenarian, element in Montanist prophecy would be comparable to that in the Apocalypse. Montanist prophets seem to have spoken in the name of "the Lord God the Father" or "the Paraclete," "the Spirit," rather than in that of the Risen Lord,[20] but this would have analogies in the prophecy of Agabus (Acts 21:11) and even, though not most characteristically, in the Apocalypse. There is some question whether Montanist speech was intelligible, for Eusebius's anonymous author reports that Montanus "began to babble and utter strange sounds" (*H. E.* V. 16. 7), which would seem to be categorized, in the Pauline fashion, with tongues rather than with prophecy. Yet intelligible "prophecies" survive; Tertullian reports on a woman prophet who both "converses with angels" (*De Anima* 9, cf. 1 Cor. 13:1), and also reports and interprets to her church; and it must be difficult to exclude any connection between prophecy and ecstatic experience in view of Luke's interpretation of Pentecost and John's own reference to his being "in the Spirit." In view of our reconstruction of a varied phenomenon, without absolute lines of definition, it would be unjust to rule that the Montanists lacked any continuity with the prophets of the earlier Church.

The history of Christian prophecy is, in fact, a sad one. Montanism was ultimately forced into schism more because it clashed with emerging notions of ecclesiastical authority than because of unorthodoxy in its content or in its expression. Thereafter the experience of prophecy, once so important and so valued, has found little place in the mainstream of the Church's life; and it must be said, paradoxically, that the Apocalypse itself contributed to its extinction. Once prophecy is written, it is there to be read, and to be referred back to; and what need is there for any new voice when we have the established word? Yet it would be wrong to end thus on a sad note. If we are right to suggest that this great utterance of the Christian prophetic voice proved in a way to be "the last word," it is still unambiguously and consistently the utterance of *Christian* prophecy, a word spoken most clearly "in the light of the Lamb."

[20]Thus in the prophecies collected in Hennecke, pp. 686-687.

Index of Names